LONDON LANDMARKS

CARA FROST-SHARRATT

NEW HOLLAND

Published in 2011 by New Holland Publishers (UK) Ltd
London • Cape Town • Sydney • Auckland

www.newhollandpublishers.com

Garfield House, 86–88 Edgware Road, London W2 2EA, United Kingdom

80 McKenzie Street, Cape Town 8001, South Africa

Unit 1, 66 Gibbes Street, Chatswood, NSW 2067, Australia

218 Lake Road, Northcote, Auckland, New Zealand

ISBN 978 1 84773 673 4

Commissioning Editor: Emma Pattison
Designer: Lucy Parissi
Production: Marion Storz
Cartography: William Smuts

Reproduction by Pica Digital Pte Ltd, Singapore
Printed and bound in India by Replika Press Pvt Ltd

CONTENTS

INTRODUCTION

London is a city that is known the world over for its vast and varied number of landmarks. With such a long and illustrious history it is no great surprise that different eras, settlers, monarchs and religious groups have all left their legacy in the form of bricks and mortar. Architecture can be one of the defining characteristics of a civilisation and buildings can come about through egotism, necessity, worship, remembrance or even greed. There are examples in this book of structures borne from virtually every desire or motivation over a time-span of many hundreds of years.

AN ANCIENT CITY

It is hard to determine when London was first settled permanently but the Romans established a town here around the year of AD50. From that moment on, people of nobility or importance wanted to leave their mark on the city. Though tales of battleground heroics and masterful leadership can survive the generations orally, nothing quite lends stature to the perceived greatness of an individual like an impenetrable fortress, a memorial in their likeness or name, or a building of their ordering. Throughout the ages, a succession of monarchs, philanthropists, politicians and military leaders has commissioned ever more ambitious projects in order to protect their territory against invading armies or to leave a lasting imprint on the city skyline that will forever be associated with their reign, work or life. William I was responsible for the first stages of the Tower of London, Henry III rebuilt Westminster Abbey, the Earl of Shaftesbury is immortalised by Eros in Piccadilly, whilst a statue of Admiral Nelson stands atop a column that is 46 metres high.

However, not all great landmarks are directly related to the life or work of an individual. Many of the finest buildings in London exist for the sole purpose of education, leisure or cultural pursuits. These buildings have come to represent much more than the facades that make them so recognisable: they are public spaces that aim to enlighten visitors. These are landmarks which have surpassed their obvious architectural merits and have gone one step further in that what lies inside is as remarkable, if not more so, than the fabric of the exterior of the building. Tate Britain, The Natural History Museum and the British Museum are just some of the remarkable London landmarks that house great collections of art, artefacts and antiquities.

WHAT IS A LANDMARK?

It would be impossible to create a definitive list of characteristics that transforms a building into a landmark. There are obviously a number of tangible features that elevate certain structures to become better known, more loved, more visited and more enduring than others. History has a keen role to play but it is by no means the decisive factor in the creation of a landmark. Contemporary galleries, spaces and structures are just as likely to take on the landmark mantle as those which have been standing for hundreds of years. However, history does have the advantage of ensuring the longevity of a building and establishing its importance in the landscape of a city. The rich combination of a fascinating history that is linked to a building of great architectural significance can result in the building achieving a certain status and recognition, which inextricably links it to its geographical location. Tower Bridge, Buckingham Palace, Marble Arch and Big Ben are just some examples of landmarks that can be removed from their London context and yet remain iconic images of the city. They are instantly recognised the world over and almost act as emblems for the city in which they stand. However,

contemporary landmarks such as Tate Modern and the London Eye are now just as likely to represent London, so great has been their impact on the capital and so meteoric their rise to the accolade of landmark. A landmark connects with an individual on a greater level than mere interest or diversion: it evokes some kind of emotional reaction. While many buildings are impressive in terms of their size, stature, age, architectural merit or historical context, landmarks also create lasting memories. They are structures of such social or cultural importance that they can have a profound affect on visitors for an infinite number of reasons.

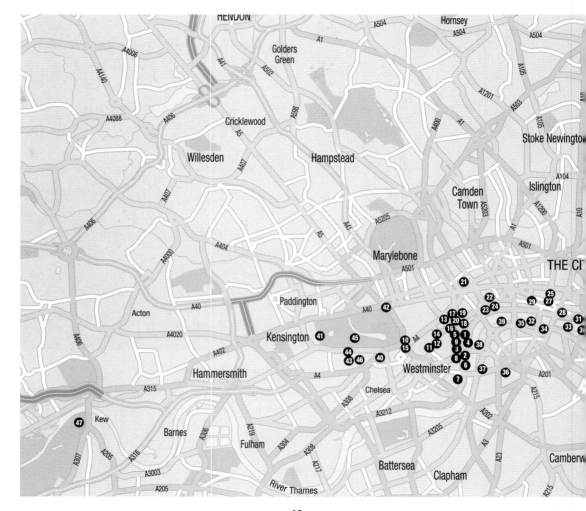

Whitehall and Westminster
1. Banqueting House
2. Big Ben
3. Cabinet War Rooms
4. The Cenotaph
5. Horse Guards Parade
6. Houses of Parliament
7. Tate Britain
8. Westminster Abbey
9. Whitehall and Downing Street

Piccadilly and St James
10. Apsley House
11. Buckingham Palace
12. Clarence House
13. Eros statue
14. St. James's Palace
15. Wellington Arch

Trafalgar Square
16. Admiralty Arch
17. National Gallery
18. Nelson's Column
19. St. Martin in the Fields
20. Trafalgar Square

Bloomsbury, Holborn and Strand
21. British Museum
22. Royal Courts of Justice
23. Somerset House
24. Temple Church

City and East London
25. Bank of England
26. Canary Wharf Tower
27. Mansion House
28. Monument
29. St Paul's Cathedral
30. Tower Bridge
31. Tower of London

Southwark and Bankside
32. Globe Theatre
33. HMS Belfast
34. Southwark Cathedral
35. Tate Modern

South Bank and Lambeth
36. Imperial War Museum
37. Lambeth Palace
38. London Eye
39. OXO Tower

Kensington, Mayfair and Knightsbridge
40. Harrods
41. Kensington Palace
42. Marble Arch
43. Natural History Museum
44. Royal Albert Hall and Memorial
45. Serpentine
46. Victoria and Albert Museum

Further Afield
47. Kew Gardens
48. National Maritime Museum
49. Old Royal Naval College
50. Royal Observatory

WHITEHALL AND WESTMINSTER

With obvious links to Parliament, Royalty and religion, Whitehall and Westminster are at the top of every visitor's list of London destinations. The area is crammed full of wonderful historic buildings that tell the story of the evolution of both the capital and the United Kingdom. The Houses of Parliament and Big Ben dominate the north bank of the River Thames, whilst the Cabinet War Rooms provide a sombre yet fascinating insight into the part London played in the Second World War. Just a short walk along the riverbank brings you to Tate Britain and one of the most exciting and important art collections in the country.

While you're there...

Wander past the policing nerve centre of London at Scotland Yard, pack a picnic and head to St James's Park, which is one of the prettiest and most popular parks in London, or hop on one of the many sightseeing boats at Westminster Pier for a leisurely cruise along the Thames.

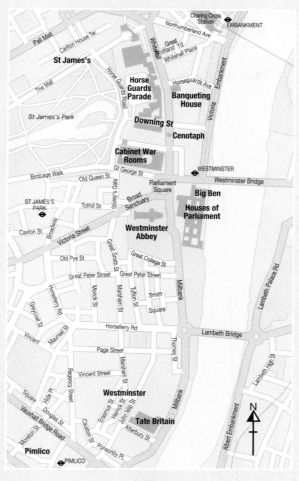

BANQUETING HOUSE

BANQUETING HOUSE IN WHITEHALL IS ALL that remains of the Palace of Whitehall. When it was built in 1622 it was a pioneering building that paved the way for a new wave in British architectural style and execution. This comes as no great surprise when you consider that the architect for the project was none other than Inigo Jones. This British architect was innovative and helped to further the practise in Britain a great deal during his career. As one of the first of his countrymen to study the discipline in Italy, Jones was undoubtedly considered to be at the forefront of cutting-edge architectural practise on his return. He incorporated Italian Renaissance design into much of his work and Banqueting House is a classic example of how Jones included his knowledge and passion in his buildings. However, the site of Banqueting House had a long and illustrious history even before Inigo Jones saw his ideas come to fruition.

Although the area of land has long been occupied by palaces and great houses, the original building on the site was called York Place. Back in the fourteenth century, this residence was reserved for those who held the most important posts in the Church. By ensuring their close proximity to his own residence, the King could converse with them on a regular basis and their comfort was considered a top priority. As the century progressed, York Place remained the home of esteemed churchmen, with perhaps the most famous resident being Cardinal Wolsey. When he fell out of favour with King Henry VIII, York Place was taken from him and the King began a series of expansion and modernisation works and York Place became Whitehall.

The addition of the Banqueting House to the ever-expanding space was designed to create a specific entertaining area and, although different Monarchs took ownership of Whitehall, this allocated space was very much integral to their requirements from the building. Banqueting House has had a number of guises over the years. The first building that was constructed on the site of the current Banqueting House was only ever supposed to be temporary but it remained standing for 25 years, until King James I took it upon himself to commission something a little grander and more enduring. When a fire destroyed his beloved Banqueting House in 1619, he commissioned a replacement straight away and this signified the relationship between Inigo Jones and the Banqueting House that remains standing to this day. Whilst the building was still undergoing its finishing touches, it hosted the first of many grand parties, or masques, which were the popular entertainment of the time.

Banqueting House is so steeped in history that it cannot fail to be considered as one of the great London landmarks. Archbishops, Kings and Queens have lived, worked and socialised on this site for many centuries and its historical legacy should not be underestimated. Today, the maintenance and ongoing upkeep of the building is taken care of by an independent charity called Historic Royal Palaces. The pristine interior of Banqueting House is open for public viewing and visitors are treated to some of the finest art, architecture and history that London has to offer.

BIG BEN

DESPITE BEING THE MOST FAMOUS CLOCK IN the world, most people are unaware of its real name. Big Ben is actually just a colloquial term for the bell inside the Clock Tower: its official name is the Great Bell. So, although Big Ben has become the universally recognised name for the entire Clock Tower, it really only refers to the bell itself. But what a bell it is. With its hourly chime alerting those in the vicinity of Westminster that another 60 minutes have ticked by, it is a sight and sound that is synonymous with London.

As the largest four-faced chiming clock in the world Big Ben is not only famous for its iconic image but also for its sheer size. Its bells first chimed on 11 July 1859 and they have been striking the time daily ever since, bar the very occasional stoppage for essential maintenance and one or two highly publicised but extremely unusual malfunctions. Although it is such an integral part of the London skyline, Big Ben has not always been London's timekeeper. A clock tower was first built on the site in 1288 but when fire destroyed Westminster in 1834, the tower and the palace was destroyed and plans were drawn up for a new palace to take its place. A clock tower was always intended to be part of the design but the palace architect enlisted the help of the Gothic Revivalist, Augustus Pugin, when it came to the drawings for the tower.

With such a worldwide reputation to live up to, it is imperative that Big Ben is totally reliable when it comes to time keeping and this was of the utmost importance when the actual clock was being designed and installed. The designer decided against going ahead with the original idea for the timekeeping mechanism and, instead, he invented an entirely new gravity escapement mechanism. Luckily, it would seem that his decision was a good one and Big Ben remains the timepiece by which millions of people set their own clocks, watches and agendas. However, with all the modern technology that is available to us now, the idiosyncrasies of this ancient clock tower mean that the time can be adjusted by minute increments by the addition or removal of a stack of old pennies that sit on top of the pendulum.

Although Big Ben is one of the great tourist attractions of the modern world, visitors are not allowed inside. Occasional access is granted to small tour groups but by and large this great British monument is closed to the public. Instead the impressive Clock Tower must be admired and listened to from the outside. As it can be seen from many parts of Westminster and the surrounding area, there isn't usually a problem in finding a good vantage point for photographs and renditions of the famous chimes. Big Ben, or the Great Bell, chimes on the hour but there also four other bells in the tower, which signify the quarter hour. This means that there is absolutely no excuse for tardiness for anyone going to work or school in the vicinity of Big Ben.

CABINET WAR ROOMS

THIS SET OF UNDERGROUND ROOMS HARDLY looks like a famous landmark from the outside and yet the course of history was made, averted and altered in here. The name of the Cabinet War Rooms has recently been changed to reflect the intrinsic part that Churchill played in their existence and operation. The space now has a dedicated Churchill Museum and offers a more rounded experience to visitors.

Although the existence of an underground command centre might sound like something from a spy movie, the Cabinet War Rooms were absolutely essential to the outcome of the Second World War. The rooms lie underneath the Treasury in Whitehall and the location meant that Churchill and his aides could move quickly and easily between the two buildings as and when they needed to. The War Cabinet conducted numerous meetings inside the reinforced concrete space during the war and many vital decisions were made here.

When the war ended, the rooms were effectively shut up and forgotten about, left much as they were when they had been operational. It seems strange now to consider that a building with such a high level of potential public interest would just be allowed to fester. However, there were more pressing concerns facing Britain after the war and the upkeep of the Cabinet War Rooms was probably way down the list of priorities. Even so, interest in this fascinating complex was kept bubbling away and eventually small parties of interested visitors were allowed access to some of the rooms. As there was clearly a growing demand for the historical insight that the War Rooms could impart, it was eventually decided that the Imperial War Museum should take over the running and management of the Cabinet War Rooms, adding this to its remit of public museums.

The Churchill Museum and Cabinet War Rooms are a fantastic resource and one that could so easily have been left to degenerate into disrepair if a solution could not have been found. It is a credit to those involved in the negotiations and subsequent arrangement of responsibility that this London landmark is now open to the public. The Second World War still has huge resonance today and this underground bunker in central London had a great deal of responsibility for the outcome. With so many people having a direct or indirect link to the War, this is another source of information. It provides a fascinating insight into the workings of the War Cabinet and the part played by the then Prime Minister.

Today, visitors can explore a number of the underground rooms, including the Map Room, which was at the centre of the whole Cabinet War Rooms operation. The museum is like a time capsule as everything has been left as it was when the Rooms were abandoned

directly after the War. Books and charts are lying on tables as if ready to refer to, lights wait for imaginary officials to return to their desks and notepads sit ready for the War Cabinet to make notes. It is an extraordinary landmark that speaks of resilience and demonstrates the desire of the government to remain close to the people and very much in the midst of the action during the worst moments of the Second World War.

THE CENOTAPH

A CENOTAPH CAN REFER TO ANY MONUMENT that is erected in honour of a particular person or a group of people whose remains are somewhere other than its location. However, when people refer to The Cenotaph, they are more than likely speaking about The Cenotaph in Whitewall. This understated but universally recognised London landmark is the monument to remember all those who have given their lives at every Commonwealth battle since 1918.

Sir Edwin Lutyens designed the large stone monument and it was completed in 1920. It was commissioned to replace the more temporary structure made from wood and plaster that had stood in the same spot and was also designed by Lutyens. This first Cenotaph had been built quickly as a memorial for the first anniversary of Armistice Day. It was clearly never meant to be a permanent memorial and the erection of the Portland stone structure ensured that The Cenotaph would be a permanent fixture in Whitehall.

Although an iconic London image in itself, The Cenotaph has become recognisable around the world, as it is also the location of the annual Remembrance Service. This always takes place at precisely eleven o'clock on the Sunday that falls closest to the 11th November. It is a fittingly sombre occasion that marks the sacrifices made in the many conflicts that the

Commonwealth has been involved in. The service is televised with The Cenotaph providing the assembly point for the various representatives of the forces. Representatives of the state and the church are also in attendance, as is the Queen.

The Cenotaph is both a visual and symbolic reminder of war. Its prominent position in central London ensures that the realities of armed conflict and the sacrifices that have been made – and indeed are continuing to be made – in the name of the Commonwealth, will never be forgotten or trivialised. It makes a striking yet simple statement about all that it represents and the lack of excessive decoration or elaborate design gestures ensures that the message is clear and simple. Two wreath carvings sit high up on each side of The Cenotaph and many other poppy wreaths join these on Remembrance Sunday. The flags of the British Army, the Royal Navy, the Royal Air Force and the Merchant Navy stand at the front, whilst a simple inscription reads: "The Glorious Dead".

The Cenotaph represents such a great deal to so many people and it receives many thousands of visitors each year. It is a landmark that is visited for reflection and contemplation and it acts as a tangible memorial for the relatives of countless servicemen and servicewomen who have died all over the world. The Cenotaph is a place for those relatives to pay their respects but it also a place for everyone who passes to take time to pause and reflect on its relevance and meaning. It is a lasting tribute to those killed in conflict and it is so much more than simply a landmark.

HORSE GUARDS PARADE

HORSE GUARDS PARADE MUST BE ONE OF the most famous empty spaces in the world. Essentially it is a large parade ground but in terms of landmarks it is much more. This vast square in Whitehall has been an important showground for hundreds of years, being used by Royalty for tournaments and displays.

Horse Guards Parade was first used as a tournament space during the reign of King Henry VIII. With its Whitehall location and its proximity to so many key sites relating to the Royal Family and the Government, this vast expanse of undeveloped land remains a luxurious use of prime space in the centre of London. For this reason, its use is restricted to extremely important events that take place throughout the year and this maintains its status as a revered space reserved for specific occasions.

Horse Guards Parade has a number of important official buildings at its boundaries and it is these that define the actual dimensions of the area. Number 10 Downing Street lies to the south of the square, The Old Admiralty to the north, whilst Horse Guards itself is to the east. The impressive open west side is exposed to Horse Guards Road, across from which is St. James's Park. Such uninterrupted views add to the sense of space and exposure and it is possible to fully appreciate the size of this impressive parade ground as you walk across the full width of the space.

The most famous annual event that takes place in Horse Guards Parade is the Trooping of the Colour and the whole area comes alive with the pomp and ceremony of this official celebration of the Monarch's birthday. This takes place in June and, although it was originally a military parade, it has also been used to mark the Monarch's birthday since 1748. Troops from the Household Division, which provide support to the Crown, parade their flag in front of the Monarch before undergoing an inspection and performing a march past. There is a genuine sense of ceremony at the occasion and Horse Guards Parade provides the perfect location for such an important event.

Another annual ceremony that takes place in Horse Guards Parade is Beating Retreat. Again, this has its

origins in military history and was used as a signal for warring troops to return to base after a day's fighting. Although the purpose of the ceremony has long since been redundant, it provides the opportunity for the military to show off their precision marching skills, as well as demonstrate the talents of the various bands and musicians of the armed forces. Members of the Royal Family attend these events and limited tickets are available to members of the public.

Horse Guards Parade is a timeless square that has witnessed hundreds of years of military parades and Royal ceremonies. The fact that is has been reserved exclusively for a limited number of annual and one-off events means that it will always be associated with high occasion.

HOUSES OF PARLIAMENT

THE HOUSES OF PARLIAMENT IS TRULY ONE OF the great landmarks of London. Whether seen from the air, the river or the road, this stunning building is an awe-inspiring sight that never fails to impress, even breathing new life into landmark-lethargic Londoners when they pass by on their daily travels about town. The official name of the building is actually the Palace of Westminster. However it is more commonly referred to as the Houses of Parliament as it is indeed home to the two parliaments of the United Kingdom: the House of Commons and the House of Lords.

The Palace of Westminster is a UNESCO World Heritage Sight and indeed, it has to be one of the most instantly recognisable buildings in the world. The famous architect Sir Charles Barry designed the building, although this was not the first palace to be built on the site. A Royal palace was first established here in the twelfth century and when fire destroyed this, another was erected in its place. This building served as the meeting place for members of parliament but this too was also ravaged by fire in 1834.

A few parts of the palace remained intact but, in effect, the majority of the structure needed to be redesigned and re-built. Following the announcement of a public competition to design the new palace, it was Sir Charles Barry who won the commission. So complex was the design and so great the scale of the building that it took almost thirty years to complete the works. Whilst the construction was taking place, the two parliaments met in some of the repaired buildings. Both the time and monetary budgets far exceeded the original estimates but the unique and enduring palace didn't disappoint in scale or impressiveness.

Despite the lengthy course of the rebuilding, this wasn't to be the end of the restoration works at the palace. The building managed to escape major bombardment during the Second World War but a number of devices did hit the structure and caused a great deal of damage. The worst attack left the entire Commons Chamber destroyed after a number of bombs fell and fires were started, which couldn't all be contained by the fire fighting crews. A decision had to be made about which parts of the palace to save and Westminster Hall was chosen. The new Commons Chamber wasn't completed until 1950 and, in the interim, the House of Commons and the House of Lords met in temporary rooms.

Today, the Houses of Parliament is still at the very heart of Britain's political system. As well as being a building of significant historical importance, it is also a place of great contemporary importance, with decisions, debates and business taking place inside that has resonance within the country and indeed, all around the world.

TATE BRITAIN

AS THE NATIONAL GALLERY OF BRITISH ART, Tate Britain is one of the major exhibition spaces in the capital. It is also housed in one of the most interesting buildings that has become a landmark in its own right, although the treasures it houses are the major draw for visitors. The gallery is located at Millbank, just along the River Thames from Westminster, and its statuesque appearance immediately announces its status.

Tate Britain first opened its doors in 1897, when the dreams of one man finally came to fruition. That man was

Henry Tate and he was better known for sugar than art in the nineteenth century. However, his passion for paintings and his philanthropic nature led him to fund the impressive building and fill it with his personal collection of art for the enjoyment of the general public. The gallery was initially called the National Gallery of British Art but even from its early life it was more affectionately referred to as the Tate Gallery. This title became formalised when the gallery began to also house a smaller collection of modern works by artists from all over the world. This modern collection began to expand and the gallery space expanded with it until it was no longer viable for the modern and classic collections to be housed and displayed in the same gallery. The modern works were eventually moved to the new Tate Modern gallery and Tate Britain could finally revert back to the original specification of its fonder: a gallery to showcase the work of British artists.

The building itself is an elegant and ornate structure with the original section at the front of the gallery having been designed by the architect Sidney R. J. Smith. Although the building has been added to at various times, there remains a sense of cohesion and nothing has been done to overshadow the impressive entrance with its porticos, arched doorways and elevated position that forces the eye upwards in wonderment and appreciation. The riverside setting further adds to the stately nature of

the gallery structure and it is an important landmark for anyone using the river for travel or tourism, as it provides a focal point on this stretch of the Thames between Lambeth Bridge and Vauxhall Bridge.

Tate Britain has a specific aim with regards to visitors and that is to tell the story of British art. Paintings and sculptures on display date from 1500 and there is work that covers every era up to and including contemporary works by current artists. It is a highly impressive collection that gives a wonderful overview of the progression and evolution of British art over the centuries with an expansive range of works by some of the greats such as Constable and Turner. The Turner Bequest in 1856 resulted in the works in the artist's studio after his death becoming the property of the nation. As such, Tate Britain has an extraordinarily rich and extensive collection of his work, including paintings, sketches and collaborative works.

WESTMINSTER ABBEY

WESTMINSTER ABBEY IS THE MORE informal and commonly used name for the Collegiate Church of St Peter, Westminster. It is arguably one of the greatest landmarks in London and it is certainly one of the most interesting in terms of its history and architecture. The building on the site today has been standing since 1245 but there has been a religious purpose here since the tenth century when Benedictine monks gathered here to pray. Westminster Abbey is so much more than just a beautiful building: it is also the coronation church and its history is inextricably linked to Royalty. This tradition has been in place since 1066 when the coronation of William the Conqueror became the first of the 38 coronations that have taken place in the Abbey to date.

It was Henry III who commissioned the building of the new Abbey. He wanted to create a gothic church and work began in 1245 when large sections of the existing church were demolished to rebuild it to the new design. It was largely based on the European designs of the day but it also included English flourishes in order to create a truly unique building that drew from a great architectural legacy. Henry III died in 1272 and the church was far from complete. In fact, it would be another 150 years before building work came to a halt. There were problems with funding and, as time rolled on, the input of more people meant that the original design was under threat from a whole host of new opinions and ideas. Eventually, the original wishes of Henry III were largely adhered to, with only a few minor changes, and the church was completed. As the centuries progressed, the Abbey became used to the sound of building work as a number of chapels were built. Perhaps the most noted is the Lady Chapel with its elaborate carvings and decorations, which have made it a destination in its own right, within the complex of the Abbey.

As well as a place of worship, Westminster Abbey is an important site of cultural interest. With a number of thirteenth and fourteenth century paintings and brasses, there is a great deal of fascinating religious art to explore during a visit. The library contains many rare texts and collections of archives and it acts as a research centre for studies relating to the history of the Abbey and those closely associated with it. The Abbey is also the final resting place of hundreds of individuals, many of whom have had a significant role to play in the history of the country. It is so steeped in English history that it has held a literal and metaphorical place in the workings of central London for many hundreds of years. Visitors flock here from all over the world to admire the incredible architecture of the building, as well as to build up their knowledge of the British monarchy and to explore the interior of this Abbey that is such a densely packed area of art, history, centuries of ceremony and celebration.

WHITEHALL AND DOWNING STREET

AS THE OFFICIAL RESIDENCE OF THE PRIME Minister of the United Kingdom, 10 Downing Street must be one of the most famous addresses in the world. The black door with its shiny chrome furniture is certainly amongst the most photographed entrances to a house and it is hardly surprising that the door has to be regularly removed for repainting and refurbishment in order to keep it looking in prime condition for the photographers and television cameras. When this happens, an exact replica of the door is put in its place to ensure the unmistakable façade of this prestigious property remains unchanged.

Downing Street is the epicentre of Whitehall, which is the epicentre of British politics. It is the home of various government departments including the Ministry of Defence, the Cabinet Office and the Treasury. It is therefore absolutely essential that the Prime Minister maintains a constant presence here and the residence at Downing Street ensures this is the case, as it provides both a public platform and a very private enclave in the heart of the city. The road takes its name from Sir George Downing who built the original townhouses in the late seventeenth century. Number 10 is actually an amalgamation of a number of properties and its modestly designed exterior belies the warren of some 100 rooms that spread out behind the famous door.

The history of Downing Street as the residence of the Prime Minister can be traced back to the 1730s. It was during this time that the first person to hold the title of First Lord of the Treasury moved into the address. The title effectively made the bearer the Prime Minister by default and when Sir Robert Walpole took on the role, King George II gave him the house on Downing Street, along with an adjoining property. However, Walpole refused to accept the houses as an outright gift. Instead, he agreed to live there during his term as Prime Minister, with the understanding that the house would be made available to subsequent Prime Ministers. The two houses were upgraded to create one larger property and the remodelling included the creation of grand rooms that would be suitable for entertaining, as well as meeting areas and living quarters for the Walpole family.

The house subsequently became inextricably linked to the position of Prime Minister. In the early years of the job, many people preferred to live in their own homes but this trend changed and it eventually became the norm for the Prime Minister and their family to take up residence in Number 10 as soon as they took up office. The house offers easy access to Parliament, as well as providing a very public display of commitment to the post and access to many of the major offices necessary to carry out the job effectively.

Ten Downing Street is absolutely unique in that it reflects the importance of history as well as the quirkiness of some of the customs in British politics. The property was built as a residential building and, as such, was never designed to contain offices and meeting rooms, let alone spaces appropriate for entertaining world leaders. It has been developed and adapted over the years to better reflect its purpose but its special place in British history has meant that the most famous front door in the world has never been exchanged for a swanky new office entrance. The Prime Minister lives and works in a 300-year-old townhouse: that's the way it has always been and the tradition shows no sign of altering any time soon.

PICCADILLY AND ST JAMES

Piccadilly is the bustling heart of London in terms of culture, shopping and entertainment and it has been for many hundreds of years. With its wealth of long-standing and highly regarded shops and restaurants, this is the place people come for continuity of service, quality and efficiency. The landmarks here are imposing and integral to the history of the area. Buckingham Palace is one of the most iconic of London's landmarks and even more impressive as the building is as much a part of modern London as it was of the historical city. Eros Statue is a compelling example of the juxtaposition of the old and new, whilst Wellington Arch sits serenely watching over the comings and goings.

While you're there...

Take part in the popular London tradition of afternoon tea at The Ritz or The Wolseley, stroll along Piccadilly and visit some of the biggest retail names in this revamped and achingly cool shopping district. If it all gets a bit hectic, escape from the crowds in Green Park, just a few steps away from the main drag.

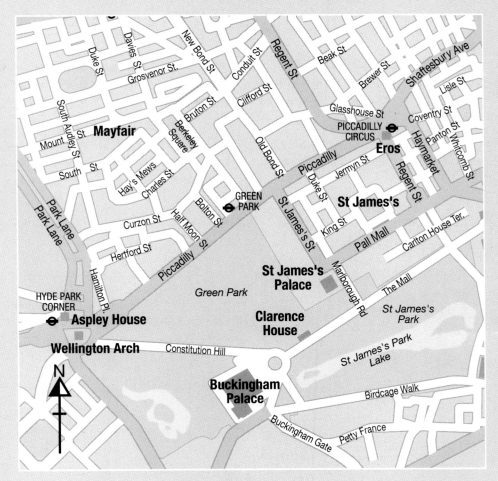

APSLEY HOUSE

THIS IMPOSING BUILDING WAS ORIGINALLY the residence of the first and subsequent Dukes of Wellington. It would be hard to miss the grand building, as it stands proud on the very edge of Hyde Park, appearing to cast an anachronistic eye on the hustle and bustle of modern London. As the world has changed beyond recognition around it, Apsley House has remained a constant architectural reference point for well over 200 years.

The stunning red brick façade provides an eye-catching contrast to other buildings and the luxurious amount of space that the house commands further adds to its grandeur and allusions to past eras. If such a structure can still produce reactions of awe in those who come to visit then one can only imagine the reception that it received when construction was completed back in 1778. The Scottish architect, Robert Adam, designed the building. Adam's father was renowned in the profession and his brother was also a practising architect so a love of buildings obviously ran in the family. Adam studied in Rome for an extensive period before setting up a practise in London and it was here that he designed Apsley House.

The client was Baron Apsley, Earl of Bathurst, and it was he who gave the impressive building its name. However, despite the longevity of the name, Baron Apsley himself was only in residence at the property until 1807. It was in this year that it was bought by Richard Wellesley and the next stage in the history of Apsley House began. The property was taken over by Arthur Wellesley – Richard's younger brother and the first Duke of Wellington – thus ensuring occupation of the property by subsequent Dukes of Wellington would continue until the family donated it to the public in 1947. They kept back a number of private residential rooms and these are still in use to this day, which makes Apsley House unique in terms of English Heritage properties.

The Wellington connection is apparent all over Apsley House with the Duke taking a keen interest in the decoration of the interior once he moved in. Members of the public are able to view the sumptuous decorations and priceless works of art firsthand and the house acts as a fine resource for the history of the first Duke of Wellington and his family, as well as the history of England at the time of the family's residence. There are paintings by Van Dyck and Reubens, as well as a nude statue of Napoleon that stands 11 feet high, by the Italian sculptor Antonio Canova and pristine collections of porcelain and period furniture.

This central London property is a treasure trove of history and relics in a family home setting. Whilst the house itself is worthy of note from both an historical and architectural perspective, it is the tangible link to Wellington and the collection of personal possessions that makes it a truly great landmark. For anyone with a keen interest in military history, Apsley House provides a wealth of information about Wellington, as well as placing his career achievements into a more personal context. It is certainly not one of the most well known of the capital's landmarks but it is a gem waiting to be discovered.

BUCKINGHAM PALACE

THE OFFICIAL RESIDENCE OF THE BRITISH monarch must be one of the most photographed buildings in Britain, if not the world. Tourists flock to this spectacular palace in the heart of London, which has become an iconic landmark in the capital city, as well as being instantly recognisable the world over. There is something about the sense of formality, occasion and British-ness that Buckingham Palace exudes that has ensured a steady stream of visitors looking to immerse themselves in the eccentricities of British culture.

As with many of the great London landmarks, Buckingham Palace began as a much more modest residence and has been added to over the years. It was originally a far more compact townhouse that was constructed for use by the Duke of Buckingham. It was owned, redesigned and enlarged by a succession of Royal residents and it finally became the official residence of the British monarch when Queen Victoria came to the throne in 1837. By this time, the building was basically as visitors see it today. The interior has changed a great deal over the intervening years in order to reflect the changing tastes of the monarchs who have lived there and to accommodate the fashions of different eras.

Buckingham Palace is far more than a house as it also acts as the administrative centre for the monarch. The daily schedules of the Queen are arranged from inside the great building and it is regularly used for functions and ceremonies. Buckingham Palace is a constant hive of activity but despite this, the State Rooms are open to public visitors for two months of the year. This decision to open up the Palace to the public has proven to be a great success and it has allowed access to a previously unknown entity. The fact that this is a working palace and a Royal residence makes it a unique visitor attraction and further adds to the experience of seeing the inside of this treasured landmark firsthand.

Although the Palace has been added to at various times over the centuries, the result is a seamless building of breathtaking grandeur. At 108 metres in length and 120 metres deep, it is difficult to take in the whole façade when viewed in close proximity. It is only from a greater distance that visitors are able to appreciate the full scale of this impressive landmark. There are 775 rooms inside the Palace and most other buildings simply pale into insignificance when compared to this colossus. And yet, despite its size and grandeur, it retains a real sense of classic refinement. As visitors stand in their thousands at the gate and wait expectantly for Changing the Guard or try and catch a glimpse of the Royal Family standing out on the balcony, it is difficult not to engage with the sense of history and formality that is on show. The ceremonies and formalities that surround this British institution form a huge part of the country's history and Buckingham Palace demonstrates that history is still very much in the making.

CLARENCE HOUSE

AS AN OFFICIAL ROYAL RESIDENCE, CLARENCE House is a site of great cultural and historical importance in the capital. Although it is attached to St. James's Palace, it is very much an individual building with its own unique identity. The house takes its name from King William IV, Duke of Clarence, who commissioned the building of this impressive structure. The renowned architect, John Nash, was responsible for the design and building work took place between 1825 and 1827. Once completed, William IV took on Clarence House as his personal residence and remained living there for seven years. It was then passed on to various members of the Royal Family and, most notably, became the residence of Queen Elizabeth, the Queen Mother, for 50 years.

As with most important London landmarks, Clarence House has had to reinvent and restyle itself in order to accommodate new residents and emerging trends and to ensure its continuing relevance in an ever-changing society and landscape. Today, it remains an important Royal building and is currently the official residence of The Prince of Wales and the Princess of Cornwall, as well as the Princes William and Harry. In keeping with the public persona of the Royal Family, this wonderful addition to the architectural landscape of London is open to the public for a specific length of time during the year. Visitors are allowed access to the ground floor rooms of Clarence House in which much of the entertaining in the house takes place. The opulent décor and ornate furnishings have all been tastefully collected to reflect both the history of the building, as well as its modern incarnation as a utilitarian home and impressive entertaining space for foreign dignitaries. The art, in particular, ensures that visitors with a broad spectrum of interests pass through the doors. The paintings are prized and represent an important collection but there is also much to be admired in the choice pieces of furniture and the ornaments and chinaware, which have been chosen to decorate the rooms.

Clarence House is not necessarily an obvious choice for an iconic landmark: it sits quietly in the shadow of St. James's Palace and passes by the radar of many visitors to the capital. And yet, there is an understated elegance to the building that complements its historical relevance and justifies its inclusion in this book. As a part of Royal history, as a showcase of important works of art and as an example of fine John Nash architecture, this is a landmark of great importance.

EROS STATUE

THE STATUE OF EROS IS A LONDON LANDMARK that people tend to visit whilst on their way to or from somewhere else. Its iconic imagery is inextricably linked to its home in Piccadilly Circus and photos of the most famous incarnation of the Greek God of love are often set against a backdrop of neon signs or double-decker buses. This lively part of the West End is constantly buzzing with the sounds of the city and yet Eros balances delicately on one leg and manages to look oblivious to the hordes of shoppers, office workers and irate taxi drivers going about their business below.

The Statue of Eros is the prominent figure that stands atop a decorative and ornate fountain. It was originally built as a memorial to the Earl of Shaftesbury and it is still sometimes called the Shaftesbury Monument. The Earl of Shaftesbury was an important philanthropist during the Victorian era. In particular, he was a leading proponent for a number of social reforms and was particularly interested in improving the welfare of children who, at the time often contributed a great deal towards the family income. As a politician he had some sway when it came to instigating new laws and he played a large part in getting the Factory Acts passed through government. This essentially put a limit on the number of hours that children and women could work in factories and it helped to ease the ill treatment of labourers.

The English sculptor, Alfred Gilbert, designed the Statue of Eros and it is, without doubt, his most famous commission. It was erected in 1893 and immediately caused quite a stir due to the prominence of a naked figure in the centre of London. The name was changed to the 'Angel of Christian Charity' in an attempt to link the statue more closely to religion and piety but it failed to catch on and it failed to persuade the more prudish amongst the Victorians that this was a valid piece of art for such public display. However, it wasn't only famous for being so blatantly underdressed: it was also one of the first statues ever to be cast in aluminium and it was a groundbreaking piece of work in its day.

Eros has been no stranger to controversy ever since it was erected. The statue was vandalised within months of being unveiled to the public and its peak has continued to provide a tempting challenge for intoxicated revellers in the area, who seem intent on trying to scale the statue. The latest boisterous incident in 1994 resulted in the figure being twisted whilst someone climbed on it. Water and heights are age-old temptations for the inebriated and the location of the statue, close to some of the main bar and club districts in London was always going to mean that Eros would not be left in peace. However, its central and outdoors location has also helped to ensure its notoriety and its status as one of the great landmarks of London.

ST JAMES'S PALACE

ST JAMES'S PALACE IS LIKE SOMETHING from a fairytale story. Looking far more like an ancient but extremely well preserved castle than the classic image of a palace, its façade conjures up images of knights and princesses, galloping horses and decadent banquets. As one of the oldest palaces in the capital, St James's provides a unique link to one of the most important and tumultuous eras in British history.

King Henry VIII commissioned the Palace and construction began in 1531. The large part of the building was completed six years later and it was a Royal residence for over 300 years. In fact, St James's Palace remains the official residence of the Sovereign, although they have chosen to reside at nearby Buckingham Palace since Queen Victoria came to the throne in 1837. The Palace oozes history from every brick and it retains an

important Royal connection to this day, very much continuing its role as a place to meet and receive important guests and to conduct affairs related to the Royal household.

The original Palace building was much smaller than the colossal collection of structures that exists today. The areas around the central courtyard were developed to add extra square footage but much remains to remind visitors of the original occupant of the great building. In fact, the main entrance appears much as it would have done during the reign of Henry VIII, with guards from the Household Division keeping watch in their distinctive red and black uniforms. The Chapel Royal and the Gatehouse are other areas of the Palace that have survived virtually intact despite the natural and manmade afflictions over hundreds of years that have brought ruin to many of the great buildings of the capital.

St James's Palace hasn't escaped entirely unscathed: in 1809 large areas of the Palace were destroyed by fire. Although some of it was restored, the impetus to reinstate the Palace to its former glory was lessened by the fact that King George III was busy making plans for Buckingham House, a building which he had purchased some years previously and was intending to upgrade to a more stately looking palace. St James's was neglected as plans were made for a bigger and better Royal residence down the road and it wasn't long before St James's Palace lost the accolade of being the home of the Royal Family. It was still used for more formal occasions but it took time before its historical importance was once again appreciated and the Palace was given the attention it deserved.

Today, the Palace is once again in use as a residence for members of the Royal Family, including the Prince of Wales and the Princess Royal. It is very much involved in the administration and entertainment side of Royal life with many important ceremonial functions taking place here on a regular and one-off basis. Its relevance today is only heightened by the accumulation of hundreds of years of significant events, residents and ceremonies.

WELLINGTON ARCH

WHILST MARBLE ARCH IS A FAMOUS London landmark, Wellington Arch, or Constitution Arch, to give it its official title, remains relatively unknown. However, this phenomenal feat of architecture and engineering compares favourably with its better-known neighbour. Wellington Arch resides at the top corner of Green Park, where it meets Hyde Park so it is almost a link between the two parks.

Wellington Arch shares a great deal of its history with Marble Arch as both monuments were actually planned at the same time. In 1825, King George IV was looking for permanent commemorations of the British success in the Napoleonic Wars and these arches seemed to present a fitting tribute. Wellington Arch has the enviable position of marking the spot where central London began on Constitution Hill. The arch provided a rather magnificent and tangible entranceway to the capital city and it remained here until it was moved to its present location in 1882. There was nothing glamorous in the reasoning behind the move and it was, in fact, as a result of road widening.

The English architect, Decimus Burton, designed Wellington Arch but the design that exists today differs greatly from the original vision for the monument. Many of the features had to be omitted or redrawn when funding for the project was reduced due to overrunning costs on the colossal rebuilding project for Buckingham Palace. Looking at the arch today, it is difficult to imagine how a more ornate design might have looked but the elegance of the monument certainly seems to be heightened by its simplicity. There was some controversy when the arch was chosen to be the location for a statue of the 1st Duke of Wellington. The statue was disproportionately large for the arch and a fierce debate raged as to whether it should be removed. It was eventually taken away in 1882 when the arch relocated a short distance away, but it took until 1912 for a replacement statue to be installed. This was the sculpture of a horse-drawn chariot that still adorns the top of the arch today.

Despite looking like a solidly constructed mass, Wellington Arch is hollow and it has a number of rooms inside. These have been used as a police station in the past but it now houses a tiny museum that informs visitors about the history of this oft-overlooked landmark. For those who discover the arch on their travels around London, there is the reward of finding a secret corner of the capital. A small balcony inside the arch offers wonderful views around the local area and the chance to step inside a great London monument.

TRAFALGAR SQUARE

Trafalgar Square is often the first port of call for those who have just landed in London and it's a good place to get your bearings and plan a route around town. Lively Soho lies just to the north east of Trafalgar Square and the frenetic pace transforms the area from media hub by day to nightlife destination by night. Landmarks are dotted around the boundaries of Trafalgar Square, with the square itself providing a big pull for visitors. Nelson's Column dominates the space, whilst the National Gallery is an obvious destination for art lovers. Nearby St Martin-in-the-fields is a fascinating church that has expanded from being a place of worship to being a concert venue, café and meeting point, as well.

While you're there...

Head to Chinatown for some authentic food and shopping, take in a show at one of London's renowned theatres, or admire the diverse range of work on display in the National Portrait Gallery.

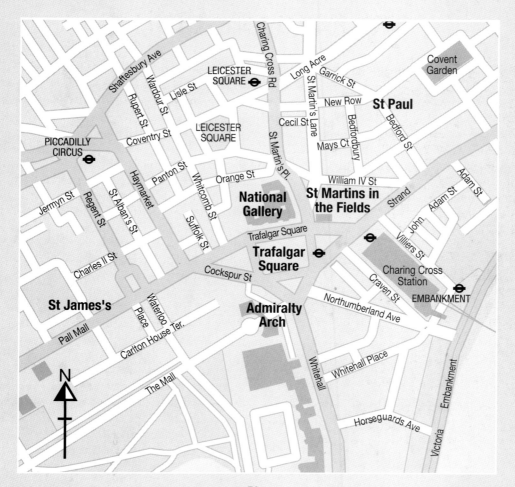

ADMIRALTY ARCH

THIS LARGE ARCHED STRUCTURE PROVIDES an awe-inspiring entranceway to The Mall, signifying the final approach to Buckingham Palace. In an area of high traffic congestion, one-way systems and tight road lanes, the vastness of the foreground of Admiralty Arch seems at impressive odds with its surroundings.

Despite its natural architectural affinity to its neighbouring buildings, Admiralty Arch wasn't completed until 1912. Although this still represents a step back in history, in terms of much of this area of London's skyline,

it is a relative newcomer. When one considers that the current configuration of Buckingham Palace had been standing proud for almost one hundred years by the time the final stone was in place on the plush entranceway down the road, it makes it seem relatively contemporary.

King Edward VII commissioned Admiralty Arch as a memorial to his mother, Queen Victoria, and it certainly does a grand job of acting as a prominent and permanent reminder. It was designed by the renowned architect, Aston Webb, who was responsible for the design of some of Britain's great public buildings during the Victorian period. As the son of an artist, Webb was undoubtedly indoctrinated into the creative arts from a young age. The functional design and aesthetic appeal of the Arch demonstrates an appreciation of beauty combined with a respect for the practise of architecture. Perhaps his father's career had a lasting impact on Webb's approach to his own discipline.

As with many of the city's great buildings, Admiralty Arch is very much a functional structure, as well as being a part of British heritage. Despite having Grade I Listed status, the wealth of space within the structure isn't allowed to simply sit and gather dust. Instead, it is used as offices, with government departments such as the Cabinet Office making use of some of the rooms. The fact that this is a living, breathing and fully functional office space allows it to blend more seamlessly into its

architecturally diverse environs. London is a constantly evolving city and many landmarks don't have the luxury of becoming relics or visitor attractions. Useable space in the centre of the city is a rare commodity and it makes perfect sense to maintain this impressive structure as office space. However, it is not just recently that the Arch has been home to the daily operations of bustling offices. When it was originally completed, Admiralty Arch included offices and residents' quarters for Sea Lords.

Despite being in such close proximity to so many great buildings, Admiralty Arch is undeniably a great landmark in its own right. Its beautiful, gently curving design, and its regal appearance act as a fitting approach to the official London residence of the British Monarch. It might not be a regular feature on the tourist trail but it offers pedestrians, drivers and bus passengers a visual treat as they drive by or pass underneath the great archways and experience a taste of London's rich and diverse history.

NATIONAL GALLERY

THE NATIONAL GALLERY IS ONE OF THE MOST prestigious and renowned art galleries in London, if not the world. It houses an impressive collection of paintings that dates from around the thirteenth century right through until 1900. With so much to explore, the National Gallery provides an almost limitless education in art history and, although the collection is smaller than those of other galleries, in terms of the number of paintings on display, it is still believed to be of significant importance due to the sheer diversity and quality of the works.

Located in the heart of central London, the National Gallery nestles up to other great historical buildings in its

Trafalgar Square location, its colonnades and domed roof striking a grandiose pose for visitors who come upon it for the first time. Although the National Gallery first opened to the public in 1824, its location has changed on a number of occasions. Once it had been agreed that there was a need and demand for a public collection of great artworks, a suitable building was given over to house the collection. However, the space at 100 Pall Mall was extremely limited and the building itself was an elegant but inconsequential townhouse that didn't exactly give a good first impression as to the aesthetic and cultural value of the paintings inside. London needed to compete with some of the other major European cities and to do this, it had to be seen to take its art more seriously and provide a gallery with a little more gravitas.

The situation became more pressing when the paintings had to be moved to a house down the road because the gallery building suffered from subsidence – not exactly the ideal scenario for the national collection of paintings. With the collection growing, more space had to be found to house the artworks. The banker, John Julius Angerstein, had donated the original paintings but it was the promise of Sir John Beaumont's collection that really propelled forward the establishment of a more permanent exhibition space. His conditions were that the paintings be suitably displayed and cared for and the pictures were given to the

gallery in 1826. Although the new premises weren't quite ready at that time, the new, much larger, collection went on display in the Trafalgar Square site in 1838.

Over the years the gallery was enlarged to cope with the additions to the collection, either through purchase or when bequeathed and it was eventually decided that the paintings by British artists would be housed in an entirely separate gallery. This heralded the founding of the Tate Gallery and the National Gallery was largely comprised of works by foreign artists. Many famous paintings adorn the walls of the gallery and visitors today can expect to see works by artists such as Botticelli, Rembrandt, Degas, Monet and Van Gogh, to name just a few. It is impossible to quantify the historical, cultural and sociological importance of the National Gallery and the treasures that are contained inside its rooms.

NELSON'S COLUMN

STANDING LIKE A SENTRY WATCHING OVER Trafalgar Square, Nelson's Column is one of the eponymous sights of London for locals and tourists alike. Its city centre position and the dizzying height that Nelson is perched upon mean necks are craned, eyes are shielded from the sunlight and cameras are tilted to unnerving angles in order to try and take in the famous landmark.

Nelson's Column has been a permanent fixture in Trafalgar Square since 1843, when building work was completed on the impressive structure. The column itself is 46 metres in height and the proud figure of Nelson adds a further 5.5 metres to the landmark. As its name hints, the column was erected as a tribute to Lord Nelson who died at the Battle of Trafalgar in 1805. Despite its simple design, the sheer height of the column indicates the great esteem that people had for the naval hero.

The landmark was designed by the English architect William Railton. He is better known for his work on various country houses and churches but his design for the column in Trafalgar Square was a firm favourite and he won the competition with it. This must have been an especially sweet victory, as Railton had failed to make a successful bid with his design for the Houses of Parliament, coming fourth in the competition on that occasion. Although hardly as prestigious or expansive a project, Nelson's Column is nonetheless as well known a landmark as the beautiful palace on the bank of the River Thames and his work is on permanent public display.

The landmark is made up of a number of different elements: the column itself is granite, whilst the plaques around the base and the leaf detailing at the top of the column are made from bronze. Nelson is carved from sandstone and the sculpture was the work of Edward Hodges Baily, whose specialism of carving ships' figureheads made him an apt choice for the job of portraying Nelson. As well as Nelson's Column, Baily also produced work for Marble Arch and sculptures for Buckingham Palace.

Lord Nelson is one of the great figures of British history but Nelson's Column undoubtedly helps to keep him in the public conscience to a greater extent. He stands proud and tall, very much a part of the modern city and yet somehow also quite far removed. His likeness is seen by thousands of people every day as they pass around and through Trafalgar Square, lingering or rushing past, depending on the nature of their journey.

ST MARTIN-IN-THE-FIELDS

THERE ARE REFERENCES RELATING TO A church on the site of St Martin-in-the-Fields from back in 1222, however, the church itself was probably there from further back in history. It is impossible to know exactly how long this corner of Trafalgar Square has been used as a place of worship but what is certain is that it is an ancient worship site that is still being used for the same purpose today.

Although the area surrounding Trafalgar Square is one of the busiest in central London, in terms of the pedestrians and motor traffic that pass in and around it, we don't have to go back too far in history to the time when it was actually a fairly remote area, with lots of open grassland abounding. This is how the church came by its name – it was quite literally surrounded by fields – and when the existing building was rebuilt in 1542 under the reign of Henry VIII, it was in a rural setting. It has enjoyed a prominent place in the history books since this time but it was still to undergo further facelifts before it would be recognisable as the St Martin-in-the-Fields that we know today.

The church was rebuilt once more in the early eighteenth century and the design proved to be controversial, although it did eventually find favour. It was the work of the esteemed architect James Gibb and St Martin-in-the-Fields was perhaps his most renowned project. The distinctive rectangular design proved to be an inspiration to architects around the world and the layout was much replicated particularly in America. More recently, St Martin-in-the-Fields has undergone a massive refurbishment project, which has seen its famous crypt café revamped into a stylish, open plan eatery, and the church itself cleaned and upgraded with improved performance spaces and more provisions for pastoral care. The church is now a wonderful amalgamation of historic and contemporary architecture and offers visitors a more rounded experience.

St Martin-in-the-Fields is well known for its cultural offerings and its all-encompassing attitude when it comes to worship. The church continues to do important work with the local community, as well as with various homeless charities and organisations, whilst its lunchtime and evening concerts and recitals draw music lovers from all over the capital. It is a church that has always moved with the times and its open door policy ensures that faith is no boundary to the individual visitor experience. Perhaps this is the reason that St Martin-in-the-Fields remains one of the most well known churches in the capital. It is first and foremost a place of worship but it is also a vital local resource, a performance space, a charitable institution and a destination restaurant. Not many churches can claim to offer so much to so many people.

TRAFALGAR SQUARE

THIS CENTRAL OPEN SQUARE IS ONE OF THE largest of its kind in London and it has been a gathering and meeting place for many hundreds of years. These days it is used for rallies and public meetings, concerts and addresses, as well as being a popular rendezvous point.

As home to the equally well-known landmark, Nelson's Column, Trafalgar Square attracts visitors who come to see the monument, the square, or both. It provides a relaxing space in which to escape the surrounding traffic and street network for a few minutes' respite during a busy day's sightseeing, working or shopping. Trafalgar Square has been a distinct area since the thirteenth century and it was also a place of congregation and recreation back then. It has undergone a number of significant transformations over the years but perhaps the most important in terms of the appearance of the space took place in the early nineteenth century when the ideas of John Nash were implemented. He had a vision of transforming the square into a public, cultural space that was both accessible and aesthetically pleasing. Once the National Gallery was under construction, the future of Trafalgar Square was discussed again and architectural plans submitted by Sir Charles Barry were pushed forwards. These included the upper and lower levels that remain today and which are linked by the expansive staircase. This had the benefit of elevating the incredible National Gallery building and creating a wonderful frame for the structure from the square below.

Further developments in and around the Square included the fountains, Nelson's Column and the four giant bronze lions, which sit and guard the column. All of these additions have remained the major distinguishing features and most famous attractions of Trafalgar Square. The beauty of this centrally located, pedestrianised square is the luxurious nature of having such an expansive and largely empty space in the centre of London. The original purpose of Trafalgar Square has been maintained and it continues to encourage a healthy tradition of debate, demonstration and protest. Rallies are frequently held in the square and freedom of speech is very much the mainstay of the activities in Trafalgar Square with people regularly gathering to listen to speakers championing various causes.

Trafalgar Square has been a square for the people for hundreds of years and despite the serious nature of many of the rallies and gatherings that take place there is always an overriding sense of calm and repose. The relaxed atmosphere comes with the brief respite that Trafalgar Square and the surrounding area offers to anyone passing through. The uniqueness of the space combined with the great architectural achievements of many of the buildings that surround it, create a naturally relaxed atmosphere.

BLOOMSBURY, HOLBORN AND THE STRAND

This area is inextricably linked to learning and knowledge and plenty of educational institutions remain here to prove the point. Ancient buildings still earn their keep as well-used offices and others, such as Temple Church, are so steeped in history that one would have to delve far back in the history books to find a time when they were not here. The British Museum is one of the most impressive buildings with one of the finest collections of antiquities in the capital, whilst Somerset House has an historic heart but a truly contemporary spirit with its diverse events programme throughout the year.

While you're there...

Get a taste for the historical side of the law with a stroll along Lincoln's Inn Fields or let the kids run wild in little-known Coram's Fields. From here you can cross over Hunter Street for a spot of shopping or a well-earned lunch break then visit the Charles Dickens museum for a slice of literary London.

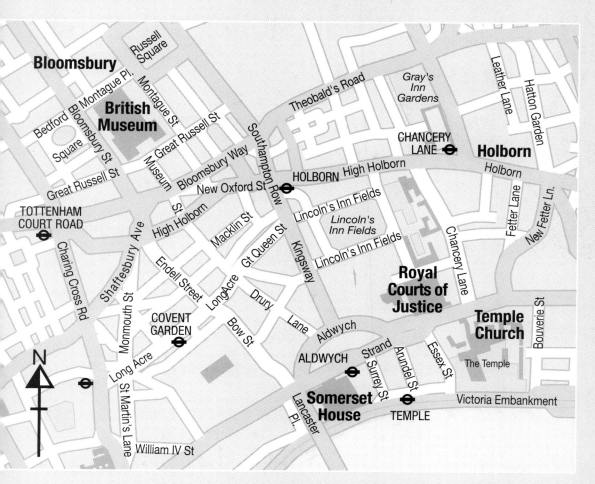

BRITISH MUSEUM

THE BRITISH MUSEUM HOUSES A DIVERSE and extensive range of artefacts relating to the evolvement of human culture by bringing together snapshots of peoples and their cultures from around the world. It is one of the largest and most well known museums of its kind in the world and it is also a major London landmark and tourist attraction, with over 6 million visitors passing through its doors every year.

The collections have increased greatly since the museum first opened in 1759. Back then it was located in a more modest building called Montagu House, which was on the site of the present-day building. Most people could only dream of foreign travel in the eighteenth century, television was a long way from being invented and other sources of information were limited so a collection of rare and insightful artefacts would have created quite a stir. Sir Hans Sloane had lovingly acquired the original contents of the museum. He was a physician and naturalist and was intent on keeping the collection together after he died and he devised a means by which this would be possible. In exchange for a one-off payment to his heirs, Sloane donated his collection of specimens and books to King George II. The 71,000 artefacts were subsequently housed in the newly established British Museum.

As the contents of the museum continued to grow, it became apparent that the building wasn't large enough to comfortably accommodate all the artefacts and the quadrangle building that we recognise today was constructed. This included the spectacular round reading room. Over subsequent years, collections of both cultural and natural artefacts continued to increase and it became apparent that they could no longer be housed in the same building – there simply wasn't enough space. It was decided that the natural collections would be transported to a new building, which would become the Natural History Museum. The British Museum continued to acquire bigger and more important cultural pieces and the collections housed within the building were renowned all over the world and indeed, had been acquired from all over the world.

The sense of space that accompanies the lavish and elaborate building is a welcome surprise to visitors. Located in the heart of Bloomsbury, this much-loved landmark is a well-worn stop on the tourist trail. However, it is not just a tick in a box – there is a wealth of fascinating information to be gleaned from the exhibits inside the luxuriously expansive building. Many of the exhibitions are permanent and attract visitors specifically to view them. One of the most famous galleries is Egyptian Death and Afterlife: Mummies, and

this is a favourite with schoolchildren learning about the ancient Egyptians. Other exhibitions are temporary and reflect the changing and evolving cultures and practices of modern civilisation, as well as drawing attention to significant cultures, events and artistic periods throughout the ages.

The British Museum has been an educational resource to millions of people over hundreds of years. As well as informing and enlightening, the Museum has become a central London enclave that encapsulates and records the minutiae of human culture from around the world and throughout the ages.

ROYAL COURTS OF JUSTICE

THE ROYAL COURTS OF JUSTICE BUILDING seems to have just the right combination of grandeur and austerity to aptly reflect its purpose. Home of the Supreme Court of England and Wales, this landmark holds great architectural and social importance for the city of London. The Supreme Court actually consists of two courts: The High Court of Justice and the Court of Appeal. These are each made up of divisions dealing with different aspects of the law.

Situated on the Strand, just north of Temple and the Victoria Embankment, the Supreme Court enjoys a prominent position on the north bank of the River Thames. The location of the Court was of great concern and debate right from the planning stages. Originally earmarked for a riverside location, the current site was chosen after a prolonged debate as to the pros and cons. The architects had been working towards designs that would complement the planned location of Thames Embankment and, in the end the plans had to be revised to fit in with the final location of the building. Although a number of architects submitted plans, only one was appointed and he was an English architect called George Edmund Street. The Royal Courts represented a monumental project and yet he was involved in every aspect of the plans, including the finishing details and ornamental sculptures. Building

work took longer than originally planned and Street died before the final stones were laid, never getting to see his masterpiece in its completion. It took almost ten years for the Court to be built and Queen Victoria finally opened it in 1882.

The Royal Court is still very much a working Court and both the Court of Appeal and the High Court are renowned for the number of high profile cases that pass through their doors. The building is symbolic of the English justice system and the laws, traditions and customs that have survived for many hundreds of years within the courts. There is a cohesive relationship between the building and the workings of the building that makes the Royal Courts of Justice such a beguiling and endlessly interesting landmark. Aside from its size – there are over 1,000 rooms in the entire building – it is the history and the ceremony of the courts that captures the imagination of visitors. Here is an historical building that is still operating in much the same way as it did when it was first built. Obviously, much has changed with regards to the laws of the land and the treatment of those awaiting trial but the essence of the activities conducted inside these venerable walls is so steeped in tradition and convention that it is almost like witnessing a historical tableau on a daily basis.

SOMERSET HOUSE

SOMERSET HOUSE IS A LARGE AND **IMPRESSIVE** building that overlooks the Strand on one side and the River Thames on the other. It seems incredible that just one structure could have been allocated such a generous square footage in an area of the capital where wealthy individuals have been vying for inches of space to construct luxury houses for many centuries. However, it was down to the ambition, determination and the ruthless building practises of one man that saw Somerset House rise from its foundations.

Edward Seymour was the uncle of Edward VI. When his father Henry VIII died, Edward was still too young to become King and his uncle made many of his decisions for him and helped himself to a number of choice titles in the process. These included Duke of Somerset and Edward felt himself deserving of a palace that befitted his newly created status. Somerset House was to be that great palace and construction began in the year 1547. It took about four years for the major work to be completed, but unfortunately for its owner, it was all to be in vain. Edward Seymour had precious little time to enjoy his new home as he was arrested and charged with treason in the same year and was executed the following year for his alleged crimes.

Somerset House subsequently became the house and playground of a number of Kings and Queens, although it was never a permanent residence for long. Queen Elizabeth I used it as an upmarket guesthouse for visiting dignitaries and then James I gave the house to his wife as her London residence. It was during this period that Somerset House (or Denmark House as it was renamed by Anne) enjoyed its heyday. It was the scene of many large society gatherings and the building also underwent a massive redevelopment programme. Much of the structure was completely transformed and remodelled until it more closely resembled the Somerset House that we know today. A succession of Monarchs added their own design features to the building over the years and the house became used to the comings and goings of new residents and being put to different uses. As other palaces took the limelight over the years, Somerset House was allowed to fall into dreadful disrepair and in 1775, it was decided that it wasn't worth trying to save the old building: instead it was gradually demolished and a new house was painstakingly constructed in its place – one which would be used for public office, rather than a Royal Palace.

Today, Somerset House is very much a public space. It is undoubtedly one of the most spectacular locations in London in which to watch live music or a film and in winter the fairytale courtyard turns into a large ice skating rink. The venue is a veritable feast for both visual and creative arts, with galleries and public spaces used for permanent and temporary exhibitions.

TEMPLE CHURCH

TEMPLE CHURCH DATES BACK TO THE twelfth century and it would be difficult to find another place of worship that is more steeped in history than this beautiful old building. It was the London headquarters of the Knights Templar, a group of solider monks who took responsibility for the safe passage of pilgrims travelling to Jerusalem. In fact, the order of monks itself was founded in Jerusalem after the First Crusade and the unusual circular design of the nave is based on the Church of the Holy Sepulchre.

The Knights Templar was a highly organised order and life revolved around the church, with accommodation and training facilities also being built on the large site. However, they also had a great deal of political influence until their demise at the beginning of the thirteenth century. The Church then passed into the hands of the crown and it was rented out to two law colleges. These eventually evolved into Inner Temple and Middle Temple and they now form part of the Inns of Court. These ancient institutions are pivotal in the process of recruiting barristers, as well as providing ongoing training for working barristers and they still use Temple Church to this day.

The building is made up of two distinct sections: there is the original Round Church but there is also a later addition, which is rectangular in shape and this is called the Chancel. The church was consecrated in 1185 and has been an important place of worship ever since. It has also seen a number of alterations to the fabric of the building, some of which have been required in order to repair damage; others to follow architectural trends or simply to give the church a redesign. Although the Great Fire of London thankfully spared the church, it was nonetheless treated to a makeover in the seventeenth century. The great Christopher Wren was at the helm of the design and the major change was the installation of an organ, although there were fierce debates as to which particular make of instrument should be chosen.

The next round of improvements came in 1841 when the church was once again brought up to date, this time to reflect the styles of the Victorian era, with brightly painted walls mimicking the original decoration of the interior of the church. It was around this time that a male choir was first brought together to sing in the church and this is a tradition that is still very much in evidence today, with the choir famous around the world. The Second World War saw the church suffer severe damage, particularly to the roof and it took a number of years for the ancient building to be fully restored. This included replacing all the wood in the church and replacing the destroyed organ.

Today, the church is very much part of the local community and London life with regular services, recitals, talks and concerts.

THE CITY AND EAST LONDON

The financial heart of London rubs shoulders with the traditional Cockney stronghold in this area that has great charm as well as grit. The Bank of England still holds great sway both in terms of the monetary dealings of the country but also in terms of its lofty presence on Threadneedle Street. The Monument provides a permanent reminder to the Great Fire of London and offers stunning views over the city, whilst along the river in Canary Wharf, the eponymous tower is a symbol of the modern city and shows how London has evolved and adapted according to its needs and means.

While you're there...

Visit the many shops, cafes and restaurants of Spitalfields Market, stop off at Brick Lane for a curry or a wander around one of the many artists' galleries. Alternatively, head down to the river for an historic walk around St Katherine Docks and Wapping.

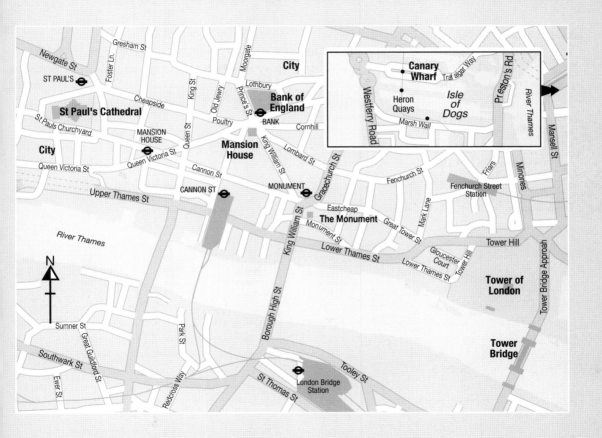

BANK OF ENGLAND

ALTHOUGH WE HAVE COME TO THINK OF the Bank of England as being an organisation rather than a structure, the home of this venerable financial institution is one of London's great landmarks. It is located in the heart of the City of London and its grand proportions and decorative stonework are about as far removed from our modern, stereotypical ideas of a bank as is possible. The sheer size of the building alerts those wandering by to its importance and it is a fitting bricks and mortar tribute to this establishment which was founded in 1694.

It is difficult to entirely separate the building from the operations of the bank itself but in many ways the two are inextricably linked. Whilst the grand old façade is a worthy landmark, it would have much less relevance to the city landscape were it not for its rich history and the huge importance that the business conducted inside has had on the financial affairs of England over the centuries.

The solid construction provides a fitting metaphor for the firm foundations and stability of the bank itself and indeed it still plays an important role in the workings of the City today. The Bank of England acts as a kind of financial foreman, ensuring the smooth running of the country's economy by creating stability in both the monetary and financial sectors. The Bank of England is at the very heart of the economy and has a direct impact on the saving and spending habits of everyone in the country, as it is responsible for setting the official United Kingdom interest rate. However, although Britons have become accustomed to the timely announcements that are made by the Bank of England, it has only held this responsibility since 1997. It has been responsible for issuing banknotes for a lot longer and, as such, this famous landmark is relevant to every resident of, and visitor to, England. Whether you visit the Bank or not, it will have a very real impact on your daily life and there are few – if any – landmarks that can make that claim.

The Bank of England rightly gives the impression of being both a venerable and hugely important building but the institution is very open about its role and operations and actively encourages public awareness. Visitors can take a look inside the ancient walls and discover the history of this great British stalwart that has helped to build and shape the economy. The building and its function provide a fascinating insight into the financial history of Britain but as a landmark, the Bank of England is so much more. It provides a firm foundation in the heart of the City, presiding over Threadneedle Street like a wise and caring relative. In fact, the Bank is also sometimes called the 'Old Lady' of Threadneedle Street and this endearing moniker is both apt and telling. She may be old but she has stood the test of time and has the advantage of wisdom and experience.

CANARY WHARF TOWER

ALTHOUGH THE OFFICIAL NAME OF GREAT Britain's tallest building (at the time of construction) is One Canada Square, most people know it as Canary Wharf Tower. Despite Canary Wharf itself covering the entire area, it is the tower that is synonymous with all financial and recreational activity in this regenerated part of East London. The Tower reaches up into the sky as a bold symbol for the huge growth that has taken place here since it was completed in 1991. It has watched over the emerging office buildings and apartment blocks in its midst, as more industry has relocated to Canary Wharf and more shops, bars, restaurants and people have moved in.

One Canada Square really signified the shift in financial and business operations to Canary Wharf. Prior to this the financial sector had been almost exclusively located in the City of London. However, with space at an absolute premium, there was a desperate need to find a new location for bank and business premises. At the time, it was a huge gamble to try and attract big-name companies to what was essentially a barren wasteland. However, with the government pouring money into the area and a transport network being established, people were slowly enticed to the emerging business district. Canary Wharf Tower proved to sceptics that the Docklands was a permanent business postcode with real potential for growth and investment.

The Tower stands a staggering 244 metres high and consists of 50 storeys. Although this is nothing out of the ordinary when one considers the clusters of skyscrapers that vie for space in many American and Asian cities, its construction was extremely pioneering for London. It was the first of its kind and it stood alone in the centre of Canary Wharf. Today, other skyscrapers have joined it but One Canada Square still nudges its distinctive pyramid-shaped roof above its neighbours.

The area has gone from strength to strength and is now not only a desirable place to work, but also to live. The landscape has changed irrevocably since it was first earmarked as having huge development potential in the 1980s. It continues to alter as more buildings are slotted into the ever-decreasing free space. However, Canary Wharf Tower has been standing proud for twenty years, its aircraft warning light acting as a focal point for the surrounding area and a kind of pulse for the manic business activities taking place inside the building.

Canary Wharf Tower has become a London landmark for being the tallest building in Britain at the time of construction but also for what it represents. London is an ever-changing and evolving city that must adapt to suit the growing needs of the people and businesses that live and work there. Canary Wharf Tower reflects the success of the redevelopment of the whole area.

MANSION HOUSE

AS THE OFFICIAL RESIDENCE OF THE LORD Mayor of the City of London, Mansion House is quite an impressive building. It is situated in the heart of the City, close to the underground station of the same name, and is surrounded by some major financial institutions and other City landmarks. The glorious Georgian palace is a suitable base for the prestigious Lord Mayor office and it houses both the private quarters of the Mayor, as well as vast areas of entertaining space and offices relating to the work of the Lord Mayor and his team.

The first Lord Mayor to move into Mansion House was Sir Crispin Gascoigne in 1752. Prior to this date, Lord Mayors lived and worked from their own private residences with some of them having offices at various livery halls. However, it was decided that a more permanent address was required for the work involved in the post. Mansion House was commissioned to operate as both a residence and a place in which the Lord Mayor could really show off the pomp and ceremony of his office and the City of London. There would be no denying the grandeur of the address on its completion, with its grand, sweeping exterior and luxuriously fitted out interior, complete with fine furniture, antiques and artwork.

Today, Mansion House fulfils much the same criteria as it did over two hundred years ago. The magnificent rooms are used for formal banquets and celebrations, whilst the offices are busy with the day-to-day running of the Lord Mayor's duties and appointments. It is a busy schedule that sees the Lord Mayor travelling around the world or holding meetings in the City and entertaining heads of state and government officials. Mansion House is very much a hub of activity and a focal point for the whole City of London. It is where decisions are taken and meetings organised, which can have an effect on the City, the capital as a whole and have implications for the whole country. The Lord Mayor is essentially the London ambassador for all matters relating to financial dealings and, as such, has an incredibly important personal and professional role to play. Mansion House is at the heart of this role and it is the physical embodiment of the function that the Lord Mayor has in the operations taking place in the City of London.

As the building is used in its entirety for work and entertaining, as well as providing the private residence of the Lord Mayor, it is not open to the public on a daily basis. There are, however, various opportunities to take a look inside this ancient building. There are weekly tours of Mansion House but there is no guaranteed entry as people are admitted on a first come, first served basis and there is an upper limit to the number of visitors. If you are desperate to see beyond the majestic façade, Mansion House opens its doors to the public at the annual Open House Weekend, which takes place across London every September.

THE MONUMENT

THE MONUMENT IS SUCH A WELL-KNOWN landmark in London that it is rarely referred to by its full title, which is The Monument to the Great Fire of London. Instead, when The Monument is mentioned in conversation or type, people automatically conjure up images of the column that stands at the junction of Fish Street Hill and Monument Street, in the heart of the City of London.

The Monument is 61 metres tall and this is the precise distance to where the Great Fire of London began on 2 September 1666. Fires were not uncommon in those days but the ferocity of the Great Fire, and the damage it caused, resulted in it being remembered throughout history. It began in a bakery on Pudding Lane but swiftly spread around the City where it raged for three days. The effects of the fire were absolutely devastating and little remained once the flames had abated. Whole streets were destroyed, as well as public buildings and churches – anything that survived was made of stone, which wasn't much in the seventeenth century.

As the City slowly recovered and buildings were constructed, it was decided that a permanent monument to the fire would be appropriate. Sir Christopher Wren designed the simple, yet striking column, which was to include a winding staircase of 311 steps that would lead up to a viewing platform, from which visitors could survey

the City of London. Building work on The Monument was completed in 1677, having taken six years in total to construct, and it rose far above any other building so that it could be seen from great distances and provide a very visible memorial to one of the greatest disasters to befall London.

The Royal Society initially used the Monument as a base for experiments but it wasn't long before this idea was abandoned and The Monument was opened as a public landmark. It proved popular, especially at a time when most people would never have had the opportunity to scale to such heights or to see London from such a vantage point. People travelled from all over London to visit the great legacy of the Great Fire and to tackle the hundreds of steps for the awe-inspiring views that awaited them at the top. However, although the open viewing platform provided completely uninterrupted views, it also presented some dangers. Over the years, a number of people died after falling from the top of The Monument. Some were tragic accidents and others were suicides but when the deaths became more common, it was decided that something needed to be done and a cage was erected around the outside of the platform to keep visitors safe.

The Monument has been closed for renovation and repairs at various times throughout its history and recently, in 2007, the doors were closed for 18 months as essential maintenance was carried out. The Monument was also given a classy landmark makeover with the stone being cleaned and improvements being made to the viewing platform. It is now ready to relay visitors to the top of the column for another century.

ST PAUL'S CATHEDRAL

WITH ITS DISTINCTIVE DOME PEEPING OUT over the surrounding buildings in the City of London, St Paul's Cathedral is undoubtedly one of the great sights of London. It is elegant and grandiose and is instantly recognisable as the great life's work of Sir Christopher Wren.

The site on which the cathedral stands has been associated with the worship of St Paul for far longer than the three hundred year existence of the current occupant. It is thought that there may have been four other cathedrals on the same site, prior to the one that stands there today and the first of these can be dated back to 604AD. The current cathedral is of jaw-dropping proportions and it was built after the Great Fire of London destroyed the existing church, along with much of the surrounding area. The epic scale of the building is a tribute to the ambitions of the architects of the time and the eponymous dome remained the tallest structure in London right up until 1962.

The Cathedral took 35 years to build and was finally completed in 1710, although services were held here from 1697. The dome was the last piece of the enormous jigsaw to be put in place and it remains one of the largest domes in the world, at just over 111 metres high. It is possible to climb to the top of the dome, to an area called the Golden Gallery. From here, visitors who have braved the 530 steps can stop and catch their breath as they gaze out at the incredible views across London. Those with less puff in their lungs can loiter at the first stage of the ascent – the Whispering Gallery – that lies around the interior at the base of the dome. The name of this area comes from its unusual ability to transfer sound from one side to the other. A mere whisper to the wall can be heard across the dome and visitors are usually keen to put this theory to the test by positioning themselves at either end of the Gallery and whispering conversations back and forth.

St Paul's Cathedral is at the heart of Christian worship in the City and it manages to successfully combine its dual role of historical visitor attraction and a place of worship remarkably well. The Cathedral is open to visitors six days a week and yet, even on these days, worshippers are welcomed in for daily services and prayers. In between, thousands of tourists and visitors flock inside the famous church to admire the architecture and scale of this famous London landmark.

TOWER BRIDGE

TOWER BRIDGE HAS EVOLVED FROM BEING simply a means to cross the river, to a famous London landmark. The image of the castle-like structure straddling the Thames is one that is often used as a visual representation of London and yet it remains very much an essential working bridge, used by thousands of pedestrians and motorists every day.

Tower Bridge is the most southerly of the Thames bridges and it was reluctantly built to try and ease some of the congestion that was building up in the overcrowded East End during the late nineteenth century. Up until its construction, the closest crossing for anyone living in south and east London was London Bridge and this represented a long and busy journey for many people who needed to cross the river as part of their daily lives or commute. Many designs were put forward for the new bridge but eventually the City of London Corporation, who was responsible for the project, chose the idea of the City Architect, Horace Jones. It was a flamboyant design compared to the rather staid and serviceable features of the existing bridges. However, it also offered the basic requirements of practicality in order for larger ships to be able to pass through the bridge and travel further along the river. This part of the Thames was still very much a working port area and river traffic was heavy so the idea of swapping congestion on the riverbank with congestion on the water itself simply wasn't an option. The bridge proved to be an epic construction project. It took over 400 workers eight years to complete and it was finally opened in 1894. 11,000 tons of steel was used to form the basic structure and this was overlaid with Cornish granite and Portland stone to give the finished bridge greater aesthetic appeal. It is a bascule bridge, which means that it can move upwards in order to allow boats and ships clearance along the river. Even today, river traffic takes priority and the bascules need to be raised some 1,000 times every year. Although this does mean that traffic and pedestrian traffic across the bridge has to stop frequently, it is also a popular sight to witness the incredible arms of Tower Bridge rising and crowds often gather to watch the spectacle.

When the bridge first opened there was a high level walkway that offered an alternative means of crossing the bridge, even when the bascules were raised. However, the number of steps up to the walkway proved to be prohibitive and most people preferred to simply wait for the ships to pass and the bridge to be lowered again to continue on their way. Today, this walkway forms part of the Tower Bridge Exhibition, an interactive display that recounts the history of the bridge, its construction and the mechanisms that keep it working so efficiently. The walkway also offers visitors an incredible view across many parts of London.

TOWER OF LONDON

THE TOWER OF LONDON IS LOCATED ON THE north bank of the River Thames and it would merge into the City of London if it weren't for the small expanse of open space at Tower Hill. It is an ancient building with hundreds of years of Royal history intertwined in its fabric and it holds many of the secrets of the evolution of the capital.

Visited by hundreds of thousands of people every year, the Tower of London is a veritable warren of rooms, alleys and pathways that transport you back to the different eras of its existence, bringing to life the horrors, excitement and celebrations of the past, which have all been witnessed by its walls. At different times, the Tower of London has been used as a castle, a prison, a scene of execution and even a zoo and it is now one of the capital's most popular tourist attractions. The Tower has also been the home of the Crown Jewels since 1303, following an audacious robbery of the collection from Westminster Abbey. The Tower was believed to be a more secure holding place for the priceless crowns and swords.

The history of the Tower of London stretches right back to the reign of William the Conqueror and the building of the White Tower in 1078. This lies at the heart of the Tower of London and it was built as a defence against potential invaders, with the walls being an incredible 15 feet thick in some places. Over subsequent years and the reign of subsequent monarchs, this solitary tower was added to and the great fortress began to spread out into the surrounding area to better represent the Tower of London that we know today. Lodges, Royal accommodation, battlements, further defences, secure rooms, recreational grounds and entertainment areas were all added to the immense stronghold and it was used more frequently and for a greater number of purposes. The Tower became infamous as being the prison and site of execution for many unfortunate individuals who got on the wrong side of monarchs, especially King Henry VIII, and they included Thomas More and Anne Boleyn. The Tower became synonymous with incarceration at this time and the barge journey along the murky river to the entrance at Traitor's Gate has become a much-replicated scene in books and films, with the terror of the accused very much in evidence as they approach the gateway to their doom.

Visitors today can explore all aspects of the Tower and highlights include a guided tour with a Yeoman Warder. Often called Beefeaters, they are the guardians of the Tower and are easy to distinguish in their distinctive navy blue and red uniforms. The ravens are another unique feature of the Tower of London and folklore states that the building will crumble if these ominous birds should ever leave. With a collection of buildings so steeped in history, intrigue and folklore, such warnings are taken seriously.

SOUTHWARK AND BANKSIDE

In Shakespeare's day this area of London was an insalubrious enclave of backstreet bars and brothels. Today, Bankside is dominated by the replica theatre of the famous bard, as well as the incredible Tate Modern, developed on the site of an old power station. This vibrant riverside locale is packed full of restaurants and cafes and is fast becoming one of the most popular spots for a weekend sojourn. It also has its fair share of London landmarks, which can all be taken in during a pleasant stroll around the area.

While you're there...

Stop for a pint at the famous Anchor pub on the riverbank and find out how justice was dealt out in yesteryear with a visit to The Clink museum. Don't miss Borough Market at the weekend: the biggest and best farmers' market in the capital.

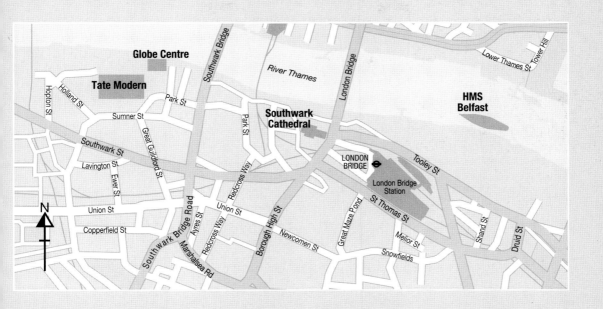

Globe Centre

Tate Modern

River Thames

Southwark Bridge

London Bridge

HMS Belfast

Lower Thames St

Tower Hill

Hopton St

Holland St

Park St

Sumner St

Great Guildford St

Southwark St

Lavington St

Ewer St

Union St

Copperfield St

Park St

Southwark Cathedral

Redcross Way

Southwark Bridge Road

Ayres St

Redcross Way

Marshalsea Rd

Union St

Borough High St

Newcomen St

Great Maze Pond

LONDON BRIDGE

London Bridge Station

Tooley St

St Thomas St

Mellor St

Snowfields

Shand St

Druid St

N

GLOBE THEATRE

THE GLOBE THEATRE IS AN ACCURATE reproduction of the original theatre that stood a few hundred metres away. Well, it is accurate as it can be: the original theatre was built from timber and it took a painstaking process of research and calculated reasoning to work out the dimensions for the new building. The original building was completed in 1599 and was owned by William Shakespeare's theatrical company. Its purpose was to put on plays by Shakespeare and other prominent playwrights of the time, theatre being a popular entertainment with people from all walks of life. However, the frivolity and joviality created by these plays was often frowned upon by the authorities and certainly by the Puritans. The Globe was shut down in 1642 and was later demolished to create more space for housing.

Despite the worldwide renown of Shakespeare, it would take over three hundred years before a replica theatre was erected in his name and in the same area where he lived, worked and saw his plays performed. It is largely thanks to the American Sam Wanamaker that the new Globe Theatre stands today. There's an old saying that you 'can't see the wood for the trees' and it would seem that Shakespeare was so entrenched in the British literary, educational and cultural psyches that we simply didn't appreciate the absence of a theatre built in the style of the original and dedicated solely to his life and work. Sam Wanamaker did

notice whilst on a trip to the capital and, upon returning to America, he decided to try and rectify the situation.

It took just under 50 years for his dream to be finally realised but in the interim, Wanamaker worked tirelessly for the project he so passionately believed in. He didn't live long enough to see the theatre completed but his dream lives on and the Globe Theatre is now a major London tourist attraction, as well as being a working theatre and an important educational facility. The Theatre sits in the centre of a larger exhibition space, which is dedicated to imparting knowledge about the life and work of Shakespeare. This is made even more exciting by the fact that the Globe stands proudly in the heart of Shakespeare's London stomping ground and it has been painstakingly created to provide a truly authentic theatrical experience. So much so that most of the tickets sold to performances are for standing spaces – as would have been the case in the sixteenth and seventeenth centuries.

Today, the plays of Shakespeare are performed at the Globe Theatre throughout the year. However, the theatre itself is also open for tours, seminars and other events, ensuring that the space is constantly used and enjoyed for a wide range of activities. The Globe Theatre has been successful in its commitment to being a warm and welcoming attraction that is accessible to as many people as possible.

HMS BELFAST

HMS BELFAST IS A FAMOUS LANDMARK ON the River Thames. Although the boat is permanently moored, her presence on the ebb and flow of this tidal river makes her appear ready for action at a moment's notice. Once a fully-fledged Royal Naval vessel, HMS Belfast is now a museum, attracting crowds of visitors to her decks to experience life on a Naval craft.

HMS Belfast is run by the Imperial War Museum, which has a total of five museums around the country. As a valuable resource relating to the historical and social impact of the Second World War, this ship is a welcome addition to the Museum's portfolio. It is a highly unusual and yet extremely informative permanent exhibition that is fascinating both on the outside and inside.

HMS Belfast is a light cruiser, which was commissioned by the Admiralty in 1936. By 1938 she was finished and was commissioned by the Royal Navy as part of the British Naval blockade at the outbreak of the Second War World. The ship had a busy working life and managed to escape unscathed until she hit a German mine in November 1939. This was not uncommon but fortunately the damage wasn't irreparable. It did mean, however, that HMS Belfast was out of action for over two years as extensive work was carried out to ensure that she was fit for service again. Whilst the ship was being repaired she was also strengthened and modernised with improvements including the fitting of the best radar equipment available. This meant that she returned to action bigger and better than before and she was deemed to be one of the most powerful cruisers in the Royal Navy.

HMS Belfast was instrumental in the remainder of the war and her versatility meant that she performed many vital missions. It is this level of active service that makes the ship so important today and the fact that it is possible to get an idea of the sheer size and scale of the Royal Navy cruisers makes such a difference to the experience of the visitor. HMS Belfast isn't a scale model or a reconstruction. She is the real deal: a ship that has seen active service over a number of years and has lived to tell the tale. Many ships of this age and level of commission were scrapped at the end of their service life. However, HMS Belfast managed to avoid the finality of the scrap yard due to the perseverance of various groups and committees. It was felt that her potential historical value as a museum ship far outweighed the cost and effort required to fit her out, transport her and keep her running.

HMS Belfast was finally opened to the public in 1971 and she has stood proud near Tower Bridge ever since. She has had to be moved from her permanent residence twice since she became a museum and this involves a great deal of planning and organisation. However, as a valued historical monument, this is a small price to pay.

SOUTHWARK CATHEDRAL

THE CATHEDRAL CHURCH OF ST SAVIOUR and St Mary Overie is universally known as Southwark Cathedral and it is one of London's most iconic churches. The site on which it is located has been associated with worship for many hundreds of years. Long before the current church was constructed, priests, nuns and the general public have gathered here to pray. There is some evidence to suggest that there was a church here as far back as the seventh century, although the first written reference is in the Domesday Book in 1068. Whilst it may never be possible to prove the exact dates or nature of the religious buildings that have called this small corner of Southwark their home, we can be sure that the Cathedral has evolved on a site that has nourished the souls of South Londoners for a number of centuries.

The cathedral was built at some point in the thirteenth century and, as with so many London buildings, its predecessor had been destroyed by fire. It was appropriated by King Henry VIII in 1536 and then subsequently rented back to the congregation until some of them got the funds together to buy it back once more. Its very existence was then threatened by the new London Bridge proposal but it was saved once more and the ancient building was instead restored and allowed to continue to serve the needs of its parishioners. Surprisingly, Southwark only received its Cathedral status in 1905. However, even more surprising than this is the size of the diocese. Stretching all the way to Gatwick airport, it is populated by an incredible two-and-a-half million people who live in over 300 different parishes.

Southwark Cathedral is located in an area of wonderful architectural disparity: the cobbled roads around Clink Street are overlooked by luxurious riverside apartments and state-of-the-art office complexes; ancient taverns ply for trade with slick, modern coffee bars; and city workers dash passed unhurried tourists. All this probably accounts for the incredibly open and accepting nature of the Cathedral towards its parishioners. Southwark has always been an area of mixed fortunes and the churchgoers were historically drawn from an extremely diverse backdrop.

The church has always been at the heart of the community and it remains so today. By adapting, evolving and changing with the times, Southwark Cathedral has continued to meet the needs of the local people and to engage them in its work and worship. At the same time, it has catered to an increasing number of visitors in its capacity as an important London landmark. A number of extensions were added to the main building in 2000 and this allowed the Cathedral to further enhance its links with the local community. A library, conference facilities, an education suite and a refectory have provided the church with more opportunities to interact and engage with members of the public and become a focal point.

TATE MODERN

THIS ICONIC BUILDING ON THE SOUTH BANK of the River Thames is the national gallery of international modern art. There are actually four galleries that form part of the Tate, the others being Tate Britain, Tate Liverpool and Tate St Ives. Tate Modern is the most recent addition to the group and it was first opened to the public in 2000 to immediate acclaim. It has since become a must-see landmark on the London tourist circuit, as well as being internationally acclaimed for its fine temporary and permanent collections of modern art.

The building that houses the Tate Modern collection is a dynamic statement that has not only given modern art a fresh audience but has also helped to completely transform this once neglected area of the south bank of the Thames. Now known as Bankside, it is a hub of creativity and diversity with the Globe Theatre and the ongoing More London scheme joining Tate Modern in the redevelopment of the area. Prior to its incredible makeover, the Tate Modern building was an empty shell that was a power station in a former life. The Bankside Power Station had lain abandoned and falling into disrepair following its closure in 1981. It was becoming an unsightly blot on the landscape and it was holding the area back in terms of gentrification. Although there were advocates for saving the building from the hands of developers keen to demolish it to make

way for housing, it was unclear as to how the enormous structure could be upgraded and integrated into plans for Bankside. Tate Modern provided the ideal scenario for the striking yet challenging power station. The industrial design and utilitarian former usage made it the perfect shell in which to install the nation's modern art gallery. The space was a metaphorical blank canvas and the interior was kept sparse and minimalist to reflect the origins of the building and ensure that the artwork remained the key focus.

The gallery is split into five levels, with a mixture of permanent and temporary exhibitions of modern art of major importance. The Turbine Hall on level one of the gallery provides an overwhelming and exciting introduction to Tate Modern, as it displays large works that are specially commissioned to fill the cavernous space that stretches up five storeys high. These pieces are often interactive and tactile, allowing visitors to engage more fully with the work on display. With such a large and imposing building being given over entirely to the display of modern, international art, Tate has again succeeded in making art more accessible. Tate Modern is an exciting building that has undergone a successful transformation into a public space and it now stands proud on Bankside as a London icon. It has been revitalised and has, in turn, revitalised the area around it.

SOUTH BANK AND LAMBETH

Cool and contemporary South Bank sits just across the river from Westminster and offers an equally exciting set of diversions for the visitor to London. The Imperial War Museum is an engaging space in which to appreciate the lives of service personnel and civilians during wartime. The London Eye dominates the skyline and should be on everyone's list of 'to dos' whilst in the city. The views are stunning and far-reaching and the experience is justifiably renowned. A short walk further takes you to Lambeth Palace, which offers an historical perspective on the area.

While you're there...

Gaze at the sea life in the London Aquarium or find out more about London's most famous nurse in the Florence Nightingale Museum. Check out the clothing and craft boutiques in the OXO Tower and gather your thoughts or unpack your picnic in Jubilee Gardens.

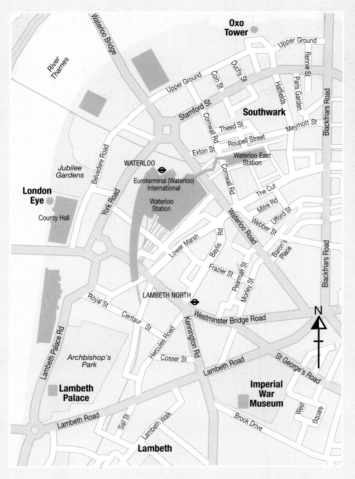

IMPERIAL WAR MUSEUM

THE IMPERIAL WAR MUSEUM LONDON IS one of five properties run and maintained by the Imperial War Museum. The others are Imperial War Museum Duxford, HMS Belfast, The Cabinet War Rooms, and Imperial War Museum North. The London museum is also the headquarters of the organisation.

Located in a substantial building in Southwark, the Imperial War Museum is an enlightening and educational experience related to all manner of modern warfare. It was the MP, Sir Alfred Mond, who originally put forward a proposal for a national museum about war. That was in 1917 and by 1920 the museum was opened to the public. The original museum was at the Crystal Palace and just four years later it moved to the Imperial Institute in South Kensington. However, this was never going to be its permanent home as it wasn't big enough to properly display all the artefacts. The museum was finally given a more long-term residence in 1936 when it moved to its current address. A former hospital, the building was suitably big and grand to house such a collection.

The aim of the Imperial War Museum has always been to tell the story of war through the lives of everyday people: people from all walks of life whose experience of war was extremely diverse. From housewives to soldiers on the frontline, it was deemed vitally important to achieve a balanced view and not just to offer visitors a selection of artefacts in staid display cabinets. Personal stories, photographs, replicas of rooms and houses all help to portray life during the war and the museum therefore appeals to a greater number of people. Veterans' families come to discover more about their relatives, whilst schoolchildren use the facilities as an important curriculum resource.

The Imperial War Museum is an interactive collection of displays that helps visitors to comprehend the many different aspects of the war. There are harrowing elements but there is also an overriding feeling of hope through education and remembrance and this is certainly not a sombre place. The atrium is a huge, light-filled space that appears to be alive with the aircraft that hang at jaunty angles from the ceiling. Other rooms lead off from this central space and mezzanine levels provide further contact with it from the floors above. Extensive grounds surround the building itself and this seems appropriate as it provides the opportunity for quiet contemplation in the midst of central London.

There have been a number of programmes of redevelopment for the building over the years but the essence of this grand old structure has been kept intact and it remains a landmark both in its surrounding area and indeed for the whole of the city.

LAMBETH PALACE

ALTHOUGH NOT AS WELL KNOWN AS SOME of London's other palaces, Lambeth is no less impressive and no less deserving of its classic landmark status. Situated on the south bank of the River Thames, as its name suggests, Lambeth Palace lies in the London Borough of Lambeth and looks across the river at its more famous neighbour, the Palace of Westminster (or the Houses of Parliament as it is more commonly referred to).

Lambeth Palace has been the traditional residence of the Archbishop of Canterbury since the thirteenth century. It is his private home but it is also his office headquarters, with the Archbishop himself, as well as his staff, carrying out many of their daily duties from inside the building. The upkeep of the Palace demands that there is a full-time staff to hand and it is vital that this important national landmark is maintained for future generations, as well as operating as a working office space and residential building. Lambeth Palace has many roles to fulfil and it has done so admirably through the ages.

Although the Palace does date back to the thirteenth century, much of the building that is visible today was built over the ensuing years. As with many of London's historical structures, Lambeth Palace has been subject to a number of major refurbishment and restructuring programmes with fire, wars and wear and tear all taking their toll on the ancient building. The Civil War was unkind to the structure of the Palace and a famous architect of the time – Edward Blore – was invited to submit plans to elevate the Palace to a residence that might better befit the role of Archbishop of Canterbury. The building was completed in the early nineteenth century. Further significant building works were undertaken after the Second World War, during which the Palace suffered considerable damage. This provided an opportunity to look at the whole building and update other areas at the same time. Today, the Palace is very much a successful hybrid of the building techniques of the different centuries it has seen. There is even a modern, glass-roofed atrium that adds a contemporary feel to the building but also manages to blend the other styles together into a harmonious whole.

It is possible to visit Lambeth Palace as part of a guided tour but these are usually booked up for months – if not years – in advance and it is therefore difficult for the public to gain entry to this great landmark. However, it is possible to visit exhibitions in Lambeth Palace Library, which is feted for being one of the oldest public libraries in the country. Otherwise, Lambeth Palace can be admired from the river and this is actually a wonderful way to view the grand old building, which has held pride of place on this stretch of the Thames for hundreds of years.

THE LONDON EYE

THE OFFICIAL NAME OF THIS ICONIC LONDON visitor attraction is the Merlin Entertainments London Eye but this is generally shortened to The London Eye, which is how the enormous Ferris wheel (or cantilevered observation wheel, to be completely accurate) is known around the world. The London Eye was never intended to be a permanent feature on the south bank and it was originally designed and constructed as a temporary attraction to celebrate the Millennium. However, the excitement that it generated meant that the wheel kept on turning and it is now the most popular paid-for attraction in the United Kingdom – no mean feat when there are so many thousands of attractions competing for the same accolade.

The London Eye was designed by the architects David Marks and Julia Barfield as a simple yet awe-inspiring symbol to commemorate the arrival of the new century. The idea was to allow people to view the capital city from a totally new perspective and the sheer size of the proposed structure would offer uninterrupted views of up to 40 kilometres in every direction. The proposal may have been simple but the engineering, design and planning that was needed to see the project through to fruition was immense. The Prime Minister officially opened the London Eye on 31 December 1999 but it would be another three months before any members of the public would be allowed to ride in the capsules. This was due to technical issues that needed to be resolved before it was deemed ready for operation.

The London Eye has 32 capsules or pods and each of these can hold up to 25 people. With a rotation taking about 30 minutes, there is plenty of opportunity to spot some of London's other famous landmarks whilst going around in the wheel. The pods are completely enclosed and the wheel doesn't stop turning but it moves at such a slow pace that this isn't an issue as far as embarking and disembarking are concerned.

The success of a new attraction can never be guaranteed but The London Eye appears to have caught the imagination of people from all corners of the globe. It isn't often that you can see the everyday from a different perspective and London is well known for its lack of skyscrapers. This means that The London Eye offers a rare opportunity to see the whole city from an elevated vantage point. At 135 meters in height, the London Eye is one of the tallest structures in the capital but the difference being that this particular structure is not only open to the public but its specific purpose is to look at London from a great height. A city takes on a whole new perspective when seen from above and for those who have lived in London all their lives, or those who are just visiting for a weekend, it is a delightful and informative attraction that is popular with all ages.

OXO TOWER

THE UNMISTAKABLE FAÇADE OF THE OXO Tower is visible from all around this area of the River Thames. It sits on the south bank of the river, in the area also known as South Bank and it is a landmark, as well as being a reference point for taxi drivers and tourists and a meeting place for locals on a night out.

The OXO Tower has a long and varied history and the original building on the sight was actually a power station that was used by the Post Office. The area looked very different back then and an industrial air pervaded prior to gentrification. When the power station was shut down, the Liebig Extract of Meat Company took on the building. As producers of the famous OXO stock cubes, it's easy to see how the name of this London landmark has stuck, even though the company moved out of the premises many years ago. The company was proud of the products it produced and the tower was going to be used as clever advertising tool. Although the letters spelling out OXO look like a classy and understated version of corporate branding, this was actually the only way in which the company could get around strict planning rules. Having been denied permission to advertise their products on the tower, these cleverly designed windows incorporated patterns that just happened to spell out the famous brand for all to see. OXO Tower was very nearly consigned to the bulldozer trucks in the 1980s when proposals were being put forward to make the best use of the land. With a shortage of housing in the area and a general sense of abandonment about the place, it was felt that drastic redevelopment plans should be put in place. In the end, however, the fabric of the building was saved and the plot was sold for a reduced price to a non-profit housing cooperative. The building underwent a complete overhaul and a sensitive development programme ensured that a community was created, rather than simply a collection of new-build apartments with no amenities. Flats were teemed with independent shops and boutiques, as well as cafes and restaurants and the entire area enjoyed a surge in usage, popularity and kerb appeal. South Bank is now a bustling and vibrant area, thanks to this development and other major regeneration programmes, such as the Tate Modern.

The OXO Tower has helped to encourage young designers, entrepreneurs and artists, as well as the residents themselves, to create a community in the heart of London. The area attracts tourists and Londoners looking for unique and unusual gifts and a more laidback and personable shopping experience. The grounds are well maintained, with a lovely park and views across the river and the summer months see an endless succession of music, art and cultural events when the Coin Street Festival takes over the waterfront.

MAYFAIR, KENSINGTON AND KNIGHTSBRIDGE

This area contains some of the most important landmarks in relation to the cultural greatness of the city. The legacy of Victoria and Albert has resulted in the great Royal Albert Hall, which hosts a huge variety of concerts and is an impressive landmark, both inside and out. The Victoria and Albert Museum encapsulates the many different areas of design and is a showcase for historical and contemporary exhibitions. Harrods is the most famous shop in the country and worth a visit for its kitsch splendour and sheer size, whilst The Natural History Museum will amaze and engage adults and children alike.

While you're there...

Kensington High Street is one of the best shopping streets in London and just a stone's throw from the major landmarks of the area. Hyde Park is vast and beautiful and should be visited by everyone on a trip to London and the Science Museum makes for another fascinating day out.

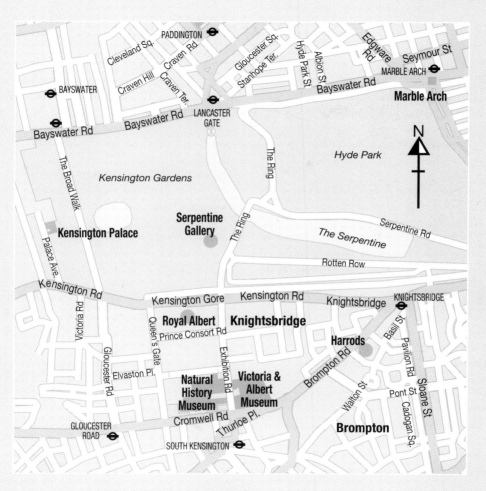

PADDINGTON

Cleveland Sq.

Craven Hill

Craven Rd

Craven Ter.

Gloucester Sq.

Stanhope Ter.

Hyde Park St

Albion St

Edgware Rd

Seymour St

MARBLE ARCH

Marble Arch

BAYSWATER

Bayswater Rd

Bayswater Rd

Bayswater Rd

Bayswater Rd

LANCASTER GATE

The Broad Walk

Kensington Gardens

The Ring

Hyde Park

N

Kensington Palace

Palace Ave.

Serpentine Gallery

The Ring

Serpentine Rd

The Serpentine

Rotten Row

Kensington Rd

Kensington Gore

Kensington Rd

Knightsbridge

KNIGHTSBRIDGE

Victoria Rd

Royal Albert

Queen's Gate

Prince Consort Rd

Knightsbridge

Harrods

Brompton Rd

Basil St

Pavilion Rd

Gloucester Rd

Elvaston Pl.

Exhibition Rd

Natural History Museum

Victoria & Albert Museum

Walton St

Sloane St

Pont St

Cadogan Sq.

GLOUCESTER ROAD

Cromwell Rd

Thurloe Pl.

Brompton

SOUTH KENSINGTON

HARRODS

IF THERE IS ONE SHOP THAT SUMS UP THE retail experience of London then it must surely be Harrods. The instantly recognisable racing green shopping bags with their famous gold logos have made their way all over the world, as people clamour to take away a little piece of shopping history when they return from a trip to the city.

Harrods occupies a magnificent building in upmarket Knightsbridge, one of the premier shopping districts in London. The sheer scale of the elaborate façade indicates that it is no ordinary shop and this becomes even more apparent as soon as you set foot inside. The huge department store is split into an eye-watering 330 departments that spread luxuriously over 4.5 acres of retail heaven. In fact, the store is so large and so diverse that tourists set aside entire days in which to explore its many floors.

The Harrods that was founded by Charles Henry Harrod in 1834 was a far less magnificent affair that was established in a far less salubrious area of London. Mr Harrod initially set out to open a wholesale grocery store that would be an outlet for his beloved tea. However, Stepney in the nineteenth century wasn't exactly a prime location with its poverty and pollution. At the time, Knightsbridge was an emerging area and its location on the edge of Hyde Park was a far cry from the East End.

Harrod set up a modest store and began to build up a reputation as a quality grocer. The shop expanded to provide all manner of everyday items and Harrod's son continued to build the business. By 1880 the merchandise and the actual premises had increased exponentially and Harrods had a loyal customer base. The Harrods name has always symbolised quality and attention to detail and this has stood the department store in good stead over the years. It relies heavily on its reputation and must continue to provide the same level of service to ensure its prosperity.

Towards the end of the nineteenth century Harrods became a public company and it surpassed the expectations of the time by pioneering the concept of the Sale and by being the first shop to install an escalator. It was also around this time that plans were made to build the palatial department store that is home to the famous shop today. The building certainly didn't disappoint in its size and grandeur and it still has the wow factor. The luxurious interiors are a world away from the stark and minimalist designs that are favoured by many other shops and this makes Harrods unique. The opulent Egyptian themed rooms, marble-topped counters and unique products and services that are available to purchase here, ensure that the store is an absolute one-off and remains a firm favourite on the London tourist trail.

From affordable trinkets that are bought to snare one of the famous bags, to priceless gems and items that most people would assume no amount of money could buy, Harrods means different things to different people. However, everyone would agree that Harrods has adapted to the many different eras in which is has traded with great aplomb. It has modernised and evolved without losing sight of the original vision of the small family firm that started it all off. Today, it is once again owned by a family, having been purchased by the Fayeds during the 1980s.

KENSINGTON PALACE

KENSINGTON PALACE HAS ENJOYED ITS status as a Royal residence since William III bought the property in 1689. Having previously been owned by the then Secretary of State and Earl of Nottingham, Daniel Finch, it was an amicable property purchase. Having secured the house, William wasted no time in commissioning Christopher Wren to work up plans for improvements and extensions to the already impressive Jacobean mansion. Several pavilions were added to the structure and the entrance was reconfigured. The newly extended house provided plenty of accommodation for Royal staff, as well as extra private quarters for members of the Royal family.

Over the following few hundred years, Kensington Palace was subject to a number of further rounds of extensions and refurbishments. There was a major rebuild when George I came to the throne but the lengthy works meant that the Monarch ended up spending little time at the palace during his reign and it was left to George II to fully enjoy the renovated house and the magnificent painted rooms within it. The Royal line continued to live, work or stay at Kensington Palace over the years but the great house had many periods of emptiness where certain rooms or wings fell into disrepair.

At the same time, the area surrounding the palace was gradually changing as well. When it first came into the possession of the Royal Family, Kensington was no more than a small village, situated at the edge of London. It was a tranquil and peaceful area, with Hyde Park as its back garden and the amenities and conveniences of the city centre a short journey away. However, as London expanded, Kensington – and many other former 'villages' – became merged into the larger metropolitan area and there was no longer a distinction between the central area and the outlying regions.

By the end of the nineteenth century the whole building had lost much of its former grandeur. With talk abounding about the Palace becoming a museum or being completely demolished, it was thanks to Queen Victoria that the Palace was saved and money allocated to the refurbishment of the state apartments. However, there was a condition to this apparently generous gift from Parliament: the apartments would have to be open to the public. Thus, the historically rich building has continued to be used as the official residence of various members of the Royal Family, as well as being a popular stop-off point for tourists and Londoners alike. The interior is as spectacular as the exterior is impressive and visitors are treated to a whistle-stop tour of the British Monarchy during the last three hundred years. With each resident adding something unique to the Palace, it is truly rich in Royal history and ancestry, as well as housing a wonderful collection of art, furniture and clothes.

MARBLE ARCH

MARBLE ARCH MIGHT LOOK AS THOUGH IT has been standing proud on the edge of Hyde Park for its entire lifetime but, in fact, it was originally located on The Mall. The arch was designed to be a magnificent entranceway to Buckingham Palace and the design was based on the triumphal arch of Constantine, in Rome. The architect was none other than John Nash, who was responsible for a great deal of the re-working of Regency London. His work was prolific around the whole country and much of it can still be enjoyed today.

Marble Arch did grace the front of Buckingham Palace for about 20 years before being moved to its current location where it strikes an elegant chord amongst the chaos of central London vehicle and pedestrian traffic. The rumour mills of the time would have it believed that the arch was moved from its position at the Royal household because the state coach couldn't squeeze between the pillars. However, this was a bit of a nineteenth century urban myth as the elaborate vehicle was just shy of the width of the arch and could pass through if required to do so. The real reason for the relocation of Marble Arch in 1851 was far more mundane: the growing Royal Family required more residential space in Buckingham Palace and the arch simply didn't fit in with the expansion plans.

Although it was a demotion in terms of address, leaving the entrance to Buckingham Palace for the entrance to Hyde Park wasn't too much of a step down for the stately Nash structure and, if anything, it was even more visible to the public and certainly far more accessible.

Although Marble Arch looks like a solid and impenetrable landmark, it actually contains a number of rooms and these formed the offices of a tiny police station, which enjoyed a central location. The police station was operational until 1950 and it was an ideal base from which to patrol Hyde Park and also for nearby Oxford Street. Today, there are concerns once more about the location of Marble Arch. It stands isolated on what has essentially become a large roundabout and there has been some debate as to whether it might be better if moved even closer to the park and a slightly quieter location, away from all the traffic.

Whatever happens to Marble Arch in the future there is no denying that it has enjoyed a rich history so far on its travels in central London. The Royal connection, the Nash design and the renown of the landmark have ensured that it remains one of the capital's must-see buildings and it will be enjoyed by many future generations, whatever its final location.

NATURAL HISTORY MUSEUM

THE NATURAL HISTORY MUSEUM IS A landmark on both the inside and outside and is equally impressive for the visitor on both counts. As the stunning Victorian building comes into view it is only right to take a few moments to fully appreciate the ornate façade and the sheer opulence of the structure. Inside the main entrance, the huge atrium reflects the scale of the exterior and this lavish use of space ensures that both the architecture and the exhibits can be enjoyed with equal enthusiasm. So often museum interiors merge into a bland canvas of box-shaped rooms and identically carved out spaces but the Natural History Museum eschews such convention and instead sets out to impress the visitor on every level.

The museum opened its doors in 1881 and it was thanks to the passion and generosity of a man called Sir Hans Sloane that the incredible displays saw the light of day. His collection of books, specimens, plants, skeletons and drawings was a rare and valuable cache and when he bequeathed it to the nation in exchange for a relatively small sum of money little did he know that he was, in essence, founding the collection of the Natural History Museum. It was originally taken on by the British Museum but there was insufficient space to display all the artefacts and it soon became apparent that a dedicated building would be needed to house the specific natural history collections. The site chosen for the new museum was originally home to the International Exhibition but the design for the new building was by the architect Alfred Waterhouse. He overhauled existing plans to create the Romanesque building that exists to this day and the famous Waterhouse building forms the main part of the museum.

The Natural History Museum holds over 70 million specimens and it would be impossible to take in even a fraction of these on one visit. It is a vast record of the world's flora and fauna that has expanded over the years as a result of expeditions, donations and purchases. However, the purpose of taking time out to go to the this incredible landmark is not to simply trawl through as many cabinets of slides as is possible: it is to take in the essence of the building, the importance of the collections and the legacy that they provide for current and future generations. The museum has been designed to appeal to children and adults alike. It provides an informative and educational foray for those with absolutely no knowledge of the natural world, as well as those who have made it their life's work. With world famous exhibits such as the replica Diplodocus skeleton that dominates the entrance hall, and the incredible full-size skeleton of the blue whale, the museum has become a major tourist attraction, as well as a much-loved and revered London landmark.

ROYAL ALBERT HALL AND MEMORIAL

AS LANDMARKS GO, THE ROYAL ALBERT HALL seems to have it all. It is an awe-inspiring building of incredible scope and beauty that has attracted performers and audiences from all over the world. Unlike many other historical buildings, the Royal Albert Hall was always designed to be a space in which to appreciate the arts. This remit extended to include conferences, talks and ceremonies but creative and scientific thinking was the backdrop to everything that went on inside the building.

Located in South Kensington, where many other great museums and galleries call home, the Royal Albert Hall was the vision of Prince Albert, who was intent on providing a great permanent public building in which people could be enlightened and entertained. Unfortunately, he died before he saw his dream become a reality but the name of the building was changed to reflect his dedication to the project. It was Queen Victoria who opened the building in 1871 and it has been a concert venue ever since. Despite its grandiose design, based on the amphitheatres of the ancient world, the Royal Albert Hall has no lofty intentions when it comes to musical preferences. It has played host to a dizzying array of classical and contemporary performers and is probably more eclectic in its musical tastes than most other venues. Its most famous event is the annual Proms and, during this time, the Hall opens its doors for eight weeks of diverse classical concerts that have been known to approach one hundred in number during the festival.

The Royal Albert Hall rises like a perfect dome from the ground and it must have been a truly visionary and groundbreaking design for nineteenth century Londoners to see. The glass and iron dome was so innovative, in fact, that a practise construction took place in Manchester to ensure that the dome would hold. It was painstakingly assembled, dismantled and then taken to its final home in London where it was put together once more, as the builders and engineers waited with baited breath to see if the structure would bear the weight of the roof. Luckily

for the millions of people who have travelled to see it since then, it has done a sterling job and it remains one of the great sights of London.

The Royal Albert Hall – and indeed many of the galleries, museums and performing spaces that were built at the time – were specifically designed and constructed as areas for public leisure. People were being encouraged to explore other facets of their lives aside from work and family. They were being encouraged to develop leisure time and an interest in arts and science in the interiors of these amazing buildings.

THE SERPENTINE

THE SERPENTINE MUST SURELY HAVE ONE OF the most enviable locations of any art gallery in the world. Located in the heart of Hyde Park, this contemporary and modern art exhibition space is surrounded by the tranquillity and green expanse of one of the largest parks in the capital. The gallery shares its name with the lake, which lies close by and it provides a wonderful interlude to a walk, or indeed the park could provide a wonderful interlude to a Gallery visit. However, despite its apparent bucolic situation, the Serpentine is only a stone's throw from Exhibition Road in Kensington, which is home to some of the biggest and best-known museums in London including the Natural History Museum and the Science Museum.

The Serpentine Gallery building is in stark architectural contrast to its contents. It is a converted 1930s tea pavilion and the main part of the building looks innocuous enough to still be serving tea and scones to genteel Londoners out on a Sunday stroll through the park. However, certain additions ensure that the Gallery stands out and there are obvious clues as to the new incarnation of this particular café. Even if these clues are missed or ignored, once inside, the transformation from pavilion to art gallery of international standing is complete and visitors cannot fail to be impressed with the scope and extent of the work on show. The exhibitions change frequently, ensuring that the Gallery enjoys a continuous flow of new and exciting work by both emerging and established artists. This also allows for a more mixed approach when viewing the work: visitors who chance upon the Gallery can pause for a short time, whilst those who have travelled there specifically can spend longer exploring the great body of work on display.

As well as housing collections of art in the more traditional sense of the word, each summer the Serpentine Gallery also commissions an acclaimed architect to design a pavilion that is erected in the grounds of the gallery. These incredible temporary structures are used to promote different aspects of modern architecture and have been used to show films, hold talks and seminars and host the BBC Proms. It is yet another indication of the excitement created by this exciting art space.

With somewhere in the region of 800,000 visitors every year, the Serpentine Gallery has garnered an incredibly loyal and appreciative following. Some of the best-known names in the modern art world have exhibited here and have either been given the exposure needed to launch their careers, or they have further enhanced their reputation by being shown at this prestigious gallery. Artists such as Damien Hirst, Cornelia Parker and Cindy Sherman have had exhibitions in the Serpentine and the Gallery continues to champion the work of both established artists and exciting new talents.

VICTORIA AND ALBERT MUSEUM

THE VICTORIA AND ALBERT MUSEUM IS MORE usually referred to as the V&A and it is an immense building which houses the world's largest collection of art and design artefacts. It takes its name from Queen Victoria and Prince Albert and it is part of the lasting legacy of the Great Exhibition, which saw a number of cultural and educational museums, galleries and spaces open as a result of its popularity and the desire of those involved in the organisation of the Exhibition to create permanent public displays of various works.

The collections in the V&A cover every continent and every conceivable medium, tracing back art and design through different countries, cultures and trends. Visitors can learn about furniture, view different fashions from the seventeenth century right up to the present or learn about the incredible 4,000-year history of glass. The artefacts merge history, sociology and creativity, which is why the museum has such a broad appeal and attracts such a wide cross-section of visitors. Art and design are revealed in numerous guises, as both aesthetic objects and also as essential tools of human evolution and identity.

The building that houses this extraordinary collection of over four-and-a-half million artefacts is one of the major exhibiting spaces in the capital. It is situated in the cultural hub of South Kensington, where the Science Museum and the Natural History Museum already draw crowds of thousands of people every day. For tourists on the cultural trail, Cromwell Road and Exhibition Road hold great significance. The V&A was founded in 1852 but it took a couple of moves before it arrived at its current site in 1857. There was already a property on the land called Brompton Park House and this was remodelled to create a larger exhibition space for the artefacts. As the collections rapidly grew and more acquisitions were made, so extra space was added to the building. The museum had a number of innovative features for its day, which included the first café to be located in a museum and it also offered late night openings in order to make the collections available to as many people as possible.

From the outset, the V&A was set up to provide a more practical approach to the whole museum experience than many of its contemporaries. There was a founding principle to try and make art more accessible to the working class and this was applicable to all establishments that were opened as a direct result of the Great Exhibition. It provided an invaluable resource in terms of education with its vast collections gathered from all corners of the globe and its fascinating portrayal of all aspects of art and design. When a new entranceway and façade was added to the museum in 1899 the fabric of the building became more cohesive and took on a more grandiose and permanent appearance. More recently, a redevelopment initiative called FuturePlan has been responsible for updating displays and modernising visitor facilities. This will ensure that this museum dedicated to design is itself kept up-to-date with the way in which it presents its collections.

FURTHER AFIELD

You don't have to stay in central London to in order to see all its magnificent landmarks: a short train journey will take you to historic Greenwich, a World Heritage Site with a pleasingly disproportionate number of important visitor attractions. The National Maritime Museum charts the naval history of London and the Royal Observatory marks the spot where Greenwich Mean Time (GMT) was originally measured. Back on the train and it's not far to Kew, where the stunning gardens have been beguiling visitors for hundreds of years. It's easy to spend a whole day here and see only a fraction of what Kew Gardens has to offer.

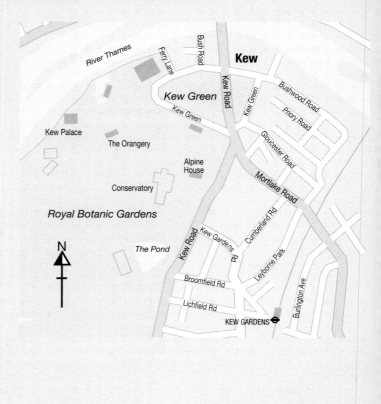

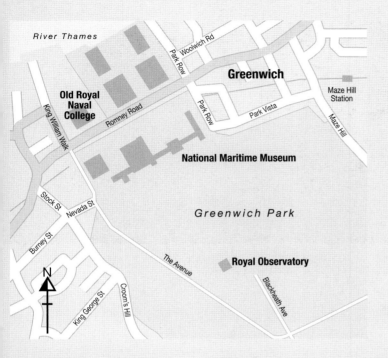

River Thames

Woolwich Rd

Park Row

Greenwich

Maze Hill Station

Old Royal Naval College

King William Walk

Romney Road

Park Row

Park Vista

Maze Hill

National Maritime Museum

Stock St

Nevada St

Greenwich Park

Burney St

N

King George St

Croom's Hill

The Avenue

Royal Observatory

Blackheath Ave

While you're there...

Check out the wonderful indoor market in Greenwich at the weekend or take a boat into central London from the pier. Get tickets for a concert at the massive O2 Arena, just a short bus ride down the road. If you're heading to Kew, stop off at Richmond for a walk in the park or a bite to eat at one of the many riverside pubs.

KEW GARDENS

KEW GARDENS IS THE LESS FORMAL NAME given to the Royal Botanic Gardens, Kew. This vast space is a carefully crafted and tended set of gardens in the south west of London, by the River Thames. This ancient area has also played an important role in the scientific research of plants and it continues to hold huge sway worldwide with regards to the work that is conducted here.

Kew Gardens is worthy of the title 'landmark' as it encapsulates the British love of nature in an area that has been specifically set aside for its enjoyment and the secrets that it holds. Whilst other areas in and around the capital have been swallowed up by residential development or retail space, Kew Gardens has retained its integrity and proven that it is a valuable educational and recreational resource for Londoners and visitors to the capital. By travelling just a short distance from the heart of the city, you can be transformed into another world.

There have been lavish gardens at the site from about the seventeenth century when the Capel family lived at the estate house. They were avid gardeners who enjoyed the pleasure of aesthetically beautiful gardens but also appreciated the need for agricultural land. As a succession of owners took on Kew Park, the gardens were extended, cultivated and new designs and areas added. Buildings were constructed for both practical and recreational use and the gardens of today began to take shape over the years. At the same time, collections of plants were beginning to be collated and cultivated at Kew Gardens, reflecting the voracious appetite of the time for all things exotic.

Kew Gardens is vast, spreading out over 300 acres and it is easy to lose yourself in the various different zones. It would be almost impossible to explore every area of the gardens and this only adds to the magical quality of this treasured space. Some zones are better known and more popular than others but there is plenty to discover in all areas of the gardens: whether you follow a prescribed route, or you wander aimlessly, discovering some of the hidden gems of the gardens for yourself. Although Kew Gardens contains 39 listed buildings, the palm house is undoubtedly

the most famous of these. Completed in 1848 the palm house was the largest greenhouse in the world at the time. It is one of the iconic images of Kew and gives its name to the zone it occupies: the Palm House Zone. The palm house signified a glorious stage in Kew's history. The vast gardens were given a makeover and the scientific work was deemed to play an essential role in the success of the Empire, with plants and seeds being sent out to the colonies.

Today, the work at Kew continues but there is a more conservation-based ethos to the research that is being conducted. Kew Gardens is regarded as being one of the most important centres for plant conservation research in the world. One of its most ambitious projects to date is the Millennium Seed Bank, which conserves the seeds from every native British plant, along with many thousands of non-native species, in order to provide a bank of seeds for use by future generations. It is this combination of preserving and maintaining history whilst simultaneously reaching out into the future, which makes Kew Gardens a unique landmark.

NATIONAL MARITIME MUSEUM

THE NATIONAL MARITIME MUSEUM MAKES UP part of the Maritime Greenwich World Heritage Site, which covers three separate visitor sites in the Greenwich Park environs. These are the Maritime Galleries (the museum), the Royal Observatory and the Queen's House. As a centre for maritime history, the National Maritime Museum prides itself on being the largest such facility in the country and it is certainly a stunning showcase for all things nautical.

In terms of great London landmarks, the museum is still in its infancy compared with many other galleries and attractions in the capital. Having first opened to the public in 1937, it is a relative newcomer but it didn't take long for the contents to make an impression on those who visited. The building itself has been around for a great deal longer and it has enjoyed a number of uses over the years. We need to look back to the very beginning of the nineteenth century for the full history of the museum to be unravelled. In 1807 the original buildings were used as a school for seafarers' children. Although the layout has changed significantly and bits have been added and removed over the years, when you approach the museum today, you are essentially seeing the same vista as you would have done two hundred years ago.

Greenwich has always been an important naval centre with its geographical location making it virtually part of the River Thames, the tidal waters lapping up to the steps alongside the Old Royal Naval College grounds at high tide. The College played an important role in the history of the town, caring for and supporting seamen until its closure in 1869 to make way for the Royal Naval College. With Greenwich so entranced by the role that water has to play in the lives of so many people, there was always a fascination with the cultural and educational side of this history, as well. There was a National Gallery of Naval Art in the town from 1823 and, once the College had been established, some space was set aside for a modest museum charting naval history. However, this wasn't of sufficient size and extent to really engage visitors and enlighten them about all aspects of seafaring.

A collection of paintings and artefacts was carefully stored until a suitable home was found and this happened when The Royal Hospital School relocated and the grandiose buildings on the edge of the park became vacant. They provided the perfect home for the growing collection of maritime exhibits and the architecture of the museum itself served to highlight the historical importance of the contents. The National Maritime Museum is a constantly evolving space and the interior of the main building, in particular, has undergone a complete overhaul in order to transform it into a contemporary, visitor-friendly landmark with plenty of interactive exhibits and changing exhibitions.

OLD ROYAL NAVAL COLLEGE

THE OLD ROYAL NAVAL COLLEGE IS ONE OF the most memorable sights on the River Thames. Situated on the south of the river, in historic Greenwich, the building is part of the Maritime Greenwich World Heritage Site and it is a building of staggering beauty and architectural splendour.

The famous architect Sir Christopher Wren designed the collection of buildings that make up the Old Royal Naval College. The original purpose of this ornate and lavishly thought-out structure was as a hospital for injured or recuperating seamen. It was a far cry from anywhere we would expect to be treated for an illness today, resembling a palace or stately home more than an infirmary. However, the fact that Greenwich was – and indeed still is – so closely linked with maritime work, exploration and pastime meant that a deserving building was required to house those who had dedicated their working lives to the sea. And so, building work on Greenwich Hospital, as it was originally called, was completed in 1712 and it would continue to care for injured sailors until it was finally closed in 1869.

The closure of the hospital didn't spell the end of the naval links with this renowned landmark. The building wasn't empty for long, and it simply changed its focus from caring for sick and retired seamen to training the next generation of naval personnel. Greenwich Hospital became the Royal Naval College and it was a training centre for officer recruits from all over the world. It operated as a college until the Royal Navy left Greenwich in 1998 for a new base and the building was once again briefly empty. A body called the Greenwich Foundation took over the management of the site and another phase of natural

progression for the beautiful building began. The theme of education continued and some redevelopment of the site took place before it opened as part of the University of Greenwich. Today, the grounds are once again bustling with students but the heritage of the building remains as it is still called the Old Royal Naval College.

The fact that the buildings have been put to practical use is important. Despite the beauty of the design, the need for practicality was always at the forefront of the brief: this was never simply going to be a structure to be admired from the outside, it had to work hard on the inside as well. Today, it is fulfilling these exacting criteria as admirably as it did when the hospital first opened. It is very much a working building that has evolved with the world around it without sacrificing its core character. The Old Royal Naval College is both aesthetically pleasing and functional.

ROYAL OBSERVATORY

GREENWICH HAS ALWAYS BEEN ASSOCIATED with history and much of this is related to its significance as a maritime town. However, it is no great surprise that the area should also be lauded as an astronomical centre of interest, due to the fact that it lies on the Meridian Line. It is this rather innocuous looking strip of metal embedded into the ground that splits the western and eastern hemispheres and dictates the exact measurement of the time all over the world. It is so important that each new day, year and millennium is officially started here. It therefore seems fitting that the site should be home to the Royal Observatory. However

the building itself had many guises before the one that stands today was constructed.

Greenwich has had a natural partnership with the sea and the skies for many hundreds of years. The Royal Observatory was originally built on its naturally elevated site at the top of Greenwich Park in 1675. Having been requested by King Charles II, the purpose of the Observatory was to gain a better understanding of the stars and planets in order to further the knowledge of navigation. This was a time when seafaring was vital for defence, exploration and trade and any advantages that could be gained from new technologies and knowledge would have been highly prized. When the Observatory was constructed, the lofty position of Astronomer Royal was also created and the holder of the position was a member of the Royal Household, which gave weight to the newly created job and proved the seriousness of the endeavour of learning more about the night sky.

The original part of the Observatory building was designed by Sir Christopher Wren and was known as Flamsteed House, after the first Astronomer Royal. Indeed, it was John Flamsteed who laid the foundation stone for the building and he lived and worked there from the completion of its construction, until 1684. Although modifications and additions have been made to the site over the years, Flamsteed House still forms the major

part of the museum and it contains rooms of astronomical instruments that have helped to define the way people have unlocked some of the secrets of the skies, as well as developed new ways to navigate the seas.

These days, we know that if we look at a clock or hear the news at a specific time, that time is correct. It therefore seems absurd to imagine that before 1884, there was no universal standard for time. It was only when there was an increase in cross-country communication and an improvement in public transport systems that some kind of international regulation

became an absolute necessity. So it was that Greenwich, with its existing form for maritime charts and maps, was chosen as the Prime Meridian of the World. From then onwards, every place on earth was measured in terms of its distance east or west of the Greenwich Meridian.

This incredible landmark is unique not only to London, but also in the world. At night, a sharp, piercing green laser beam shines out to mark the exact spot of the Meridian Line and by day tourists clamour to stand with one foot firmly planted in each of the hemispheres.

ADDRESSES

WHITEHALL AND WESTMINSTER

Banqueting House, p. 14
Whitehall, SW1A 2ER
www.hrp.org.uk/banquetinghouse
TUBE: Westminster, Embankment

Big Ben, p. 16
20 Dean's Yard, SW1P 3PA
www.parliament.uk/visiting/
visiting-and-tours/bigben
TUBE: Westminster

Cabinet War Rooms, p. 18
King Charles Street, SW1A 2AQ
cwr.iwm.org.uk
TUBE: Westminster, St James's Park

The Cenotaph, p. 20
Whitehall, SW1 2ER
TUBE: Westminster, Embankment

Horse Guards Parade, p. 24
Whitehall, SW1A 2AX
TUBE: Westminster, Embankment

Houses of Parliament, p. 26
House of Commons, SW1A 0AA
House of Lords, SW1A 0PW
www.parliament.uk
TUBE: Westminster

Tate Britain, p. 28
Millbank, SW1P 4RG
www.tate.org.uk/britain
TUBE: Pimlico

Westminster Abbey, p. 31
20 Dean's Yard, SW1P 3PA
www.westminster-abbey.org
TUBE: Westminster, St James's Park

Whitehall and Downing Street, p. 32
10 Downing Street, SW1A 2AA
www.number10.gov.uk
TUBE: Westminster

PICCADILLY AND ST JAMES

Apsley House, p. 36
149 Piccadilly, Hyde Park Corner,
W1J 7NT

www.english-heritage.org.uk/daysout/
properties/apsley-house
TUBE: Hyde Park Corner

Buckingham Palace, p. 38
Buckingham Palace Road, SW1A 1AA
www.royalcollection.org.uk
TUBE: Victoria, Green Park, Hyde
Park Corner

Clarence House, p. 41
The Mall, SW1A 1AA
www.royalcollection.org.uk
TUBE: Green Park, St James's Park

Eros Statue, p. 44
Piccadilly Circus, W1
TUBE: Piccadilly Circus

St. James's Palace, p. 46
Cleveland Row, SW1A 1DH
www.royal.gov.uk
TUBE: Green Park, St James's Park

Wellington Arch, p. 49
Hyde Park, W1J 7JZ

www.english-heritage.org.uk/daysout/
properties/wellington-arch
TUBE: Hyde Park Corner

TRAFALGAR SQUARE

Admiralty Arch, p. 52
The Mall, SW1
TUBE: Charing Cross

National Gallery, p. 54
Trafalgar Square, WC2N 5DN

www.nationalgallery.org.uk
TUBE: Charing Cross, Leicester Square

Nelson's Column, p. 57
Trafalgar Square, WC2
TUBE: Charing Cross, Leicester Square

St. Martin-in-the-Fields, p. 60
Trafalgar Square, WC2N 4JJ
www2.stmartin-in-the-fields.org
TUBE: Charing Cross, Leicester Square

Trafalgar Square, p. 63
Trafalgar Square, WC2
www.london.gov.uk/trafalgarsquare
TUBE: Charing Cross, Leicester Square

BLOOMSBURY, HOLBORN AND STRAND

British Museum, p. 66
Great Russell Street, WC1B 3DG
www.britishmuseum.org
TUBE: Tottenham Court Road

THE CITY AND EAST LONDON

SOUTHWARK AND BANKSIDE

SOUTH BANK AND LAMBETH

London Eye, p. 110
Westminster Bridge Road, SE1 7PB
www.londoneye.com
TUBE: Waterloo

OXO Tower, p. 113
South Bank, SE1 9PH
www.coinstreet.org/developments/
oxotowerwharf.html
TUBE: Southwark, Waterloo

KENSINGTON, MAYFAIR AND KNIGHTSBRIDGE

Harrods, p. 116
87-135 Brompton Road, SW1X 7XL
www.harrods.com
RAIL: Knightsbridge

Kensington Palace, p. 119
Kensington Gardens, W8 4PX
www.hrp.org.uk/kensingtonpalace
TUBE: High Street Kensington

Marble Arch, p. 120
Oxford Street, W1
TUBE: Marble Arch

Natural History Museum, p. 123
Cromwell Road, SW7 5BD
www.nhm.ac.uk
TUBE: South Kensington

Royal Albert Hall and Memorial, p. 124
Kensington Gore, SW7 2AP
www.royalalberthall.com
TUBE: South Kensington, High Street Kensington

The Serpentine, p. 127
Kensington Gardens, W2 3XA
www.serpentinegallery.org
TUBE: Knightsbridge, Lancaster Gate, South Kensington

Victoria and Albert Museum, p. 128
Cromwell Road, SW7 2RL
www.vam.ac.uk
TUBE: South Kensington

Further Afield

Kew Gardens, p. 132
Kew, Richmond, TW9 3AB
www.kew.org
TUBE: Kew Gardens

National Maritime Museum, p. 135
Romney Road, Greenwich, SE10 9NF
www.nmm.ac.uk
TUBE: Cutty Sark DLR

Old Royal Naval College, p. 136
Old Royal Naval College, Greenwich, SE10 9LW
www.oldroyalnavalcollege.org
TUBE: Cutty Sark DLR

Royal Observatory, p. 138
Blackheath Avenue, Greenwich, SE10 8XJ
www.nmm.ac.uk/places/royal-observatory
TUBE: Cutty Sark DLR